COLORADO CROSS-COUNTRY SKIING

by Lisa Stanton

Maps
Francis Stanton

Illustrations
Caron Elizabeth Dunn

Front Cover
Louise P. Stanton

West Side Press
Glenwood Springs, Colorado

Copyright © 1985 West Side Press

Library of Congress Catalog Card Number 85-40709

ISBN 0-935073-10-8

Published by
West Side Press
P.O. Box 1457
Glenwood Springs, CO, 81602

Printed in the United States of America

First Edition 1985

Contents

Contents

Contents

Contents

ACKNOWLEDGEMENTS

This book could not have been written without the assistance and knowledge of so many people. I would like to thank all those at the various cross-country centers who spent their valuable time during the busy ski season answering my questions and providing me with tours of the trails and their establishments.

I would also like to thank Sally Valin for the time she invested as my editor; Caron Dunn for her beautiful renditions of the cross-country centers; Louise P. Stanton for her talent in capturing the essence of winter in the Colorado Rockies; Jill Musser for her patience with me and my time schedule; John Fisher and the Colorado Cross Country Ski Association for their help and ideas; and most of all, Francis Stanton, without whose patience, cartographic talent, support and encouragement I would not have been able to write this book.

Colorado Mountains

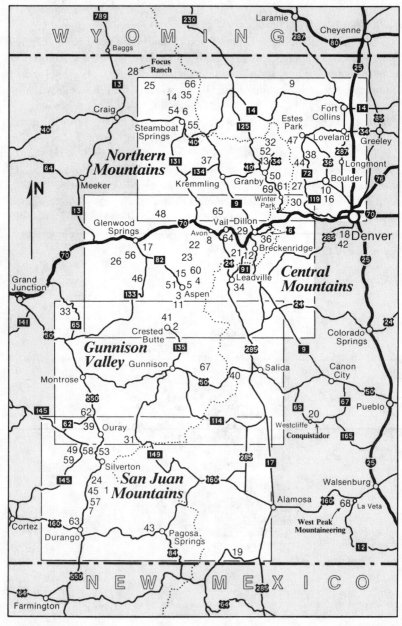

Legend on Page 15

Cross-Country Centers

This alphabetical list is keyed to the map at left and on the next page.

1. Ah, Wilderness Guest Ranch (SJM)
2. Ambush Ranch (GV)
3. Ashcroft Ski Touring Unlimited (CM)
4. Aspen Touring Center (CM)
5. Aspen/Snowmass Nordic Council (CM)
6. Bear Pole Ranch (NM)
7. Bear Ranch (SJM)
8. Beaver Creek Cross Country Ski Center (CM)
9. Beaver Meadows (NM)
10. Boulder Outdoor Center (NM)
11. Braun Hut System (CM)
12. Breckenridge Nordic Ski Center (CM)
13. C Lazy U Ranch (NM)
14. Clark Store (NM)
15. Colorado First Tracks (CM)
16. Colorado Grand Tour (NM)
17. Colorado Mountain College (CM)
18. Colorado Outward Bound (NM)
19. Conejos Ranch (SJM)
20. Conquistador Ski Area (Westcliffe, CO)
21. Copper Mountain Cross Country Ski Center (CM)
22. Crooked Creek Ski Touring (CM)
23. Diamond J Ranch (CM)
24. Durango Helicopters (SJM)
25. Dutch Creek Guest Ranch (NM)
26. East Divide Lodge (CM)
27. Eldora Touring Center (NM)
28. Focus Ranch (NM)
29. Frisco Experimental Trails (CM)
30. Gilpin County Outfitters (NM)
31. Golconda Resort (SJM)
32. Grand Lake Golf Course Ski Touring Center(NM)
33. Grand Mesa Lodge (GV)
34. Happy Trails Guides (CM)
35. Home Ranch (NM)
36. Keystone Ski Touring Center (CM)
37. Latigo Ranch (NM)
38. Lazy H Ranch (NM)
39. MacTiernan's San Juan Guest Ranch (SJM)
40. Monarch Ski Touring Center (GV)
41. Nordic Adventure/Trak Ski Touring Center (GV)
42. Outdoor Training Leadership Seminars (NM)
43. Pagosa Pines Touring Center (SJM)
44. Peaceful Valley Ski Ranch (NM)
45. Purgatory Ski Touring Center (SJM)
46. Redstone Inn Ski Touring Center (CM)
47. Rocky Mountain Ski Tours (NM)
48. 7W Guest Ranch (CM)
49. Sidewinder Ski Tours (SJM)
50. SilverCreek Nordic Center (NM)
51. Snowmass Club Ski Touring Center (CM)
52. Soda Springs Ranch (NM)
53. St. Paul Cross Country Ski Lodge (SJM)
54. Steamboat Powder Cats (NM)
55. Steamboat Touring Center (NM)
56. Sunlight Ski Touring Center (CM)
57. Tamarron Resort (SJM)
58. Telluride Cross Country Ski Touring Center (SJM)
59. Telluride Helitrax (SJM)
60. Tenth Mountain Trail Association (CM)
61. Tour Ski Idlewild (NM)
62. Uncompahgre Mountain Guides (SJM)
63. Unordinary Adventures (SJM)
64. Vail Cross Country Ski Center (CM)
65. Vail Heliski (CM)
66. Vista Verde Guest Ranch (NM)
67. Waunita Hot Springs Ranch (GV)
68. West Peak Mountaineering (La Veta, CO)
69. YMCA/Snow Mountain Ranch (NM)

(NM) - Northern Mountains consisting of the Steamboat Springs, Granby and Front Range areas.
(CM) - Central Mountains consisting of the Vail, Summit County and Aspen areas.
(GV) - Gunnison Valley area.
(SJM) - San Juan Mountains area.

Transportation Map

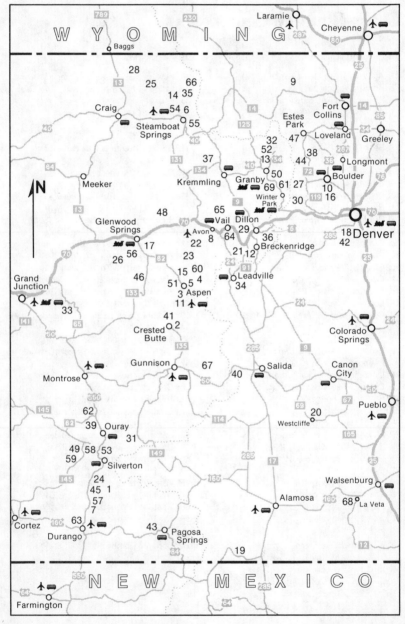

Legend on Page 15

Introduction

Colorado's exquisite skiing conditions and Rocky Mountain terrain have long attracted skiers from all over the world. Originally of the downhill persuasion, visitors are fast becoming advocates of cross-country skiing.

Cross-country skiing provides an alternative experience to the hectic and crowded slopes of the downhill ski resorts and can be as relaxing or as strenuous as you choose to make it. Some skiers use nordic skiing as a chance to tour the winter countryside in the fresh mountain air; others use it as an aerobic exercise and physical workout to tax and train their bodies and to strengthen their cardiovascular system.

Colorado's mountains offer a variety of winter settings in which skiers can enjoy such delightful challenges as basic cross-country skiing, exploring backcountry trails, competing in a cross-country race at a well-maintained track system, flying to the top of a mountain (via helicopter) to telemark down an untracked slope of powder, and later being pampered at a genuine Colorado dude ranch. These diverse activities are offered at Colorado's various cross-country skiing centers—the subject of this book.

Colorado's ski season extends from Thanksgiving to Easter every year; some higher elevations boast great skiing from early November to late May. Snowfall can average from 200 inches to 500 inches (at Wolf Creek Pass) a year, depending on location and altitude.

ABOUT THIS GUIDE

This book describes the cross-country centers in Colorado that provide the various facets of this increasingly popular sport. (The term "cross-country center" is used throughout this introduction to denote all the places and operations for cross-country skiing described in this book.) The cross-country centers we have chosen to describe, under the headings of Touring Centers and Resorts, and Ranches and Lodges, are all full-service cross-country centers and provide most or all of the following: maintained cross-country trail systems, ski equipment rentals, cross-country instruction, cross-country races, and guided tours.

Touring centers are usually associated with an alpine ski resort and often share grooming equipment, base facilities, and ski instruction with the resort.

Resorts are generally owned and run by large development complexes and, in addition to the nordic programs, include condominiums, athletic clubs and restaurants, and offer an "upscale" experience.

Ranches are usually family-owned enterprises that combine dude ranching, farming, and guest accommodations. Many of these ranches are already well-established and have recently, within the last five years, added cross-country programs to their winter schedules.

Lodges generally offer accommodation and cross-country programs, usually in an isolated high-country setting.

Also described in this book are a few cross-country ranches that are not full-service ranches; that is, along with meals and accommodations, they offer only one of the following: a maintained trail system, equipment rental, cross-country instruction, races or guided tours.

A few outstanding school programs offered within Colorado are mentioned. In addition to offering instruction in cross-country skiing, these programs help students achieve a sense of confidence and expertise in the outdoor winter environment.

Our backcountry sections cover other aspects of cross-country skiing, such as hut systems, cross-country guides (which includes heliskiing and snowcat tour guides), and backcountry trails. Hut systems offer hut-to-hut skiing—backcountry skiing from one warm cabin to the next for an extended nordic experience. Cross-country guides provide skiing and avalanche-safety expertise as well as escort service on local backcountry trails. Helicopter skiing consists of a helicopter ride to otherwise-unreachable terrain and a guided descent. Snowcats provide transportation by snow machine to upper reaches of mountain ranges for nordic downhill descents. Backcountry trails are generally Forest Service roads and trails, usually marked but not maintained. See the backcountry section later in this introduction.

CROSS-COUNTRY CENTERS

The 69 cross-country centers described in this book are shown on two maps of the Colorado mountains. The first map locates each cross-country center within four regions, and is keyed to an alphabetical list of the centers. The second map shows the air, bus and train terminals and can be used as a reference for your travel arrangements.

The four regions are: the Northern Mountains, which covers the Steamboat, Granby and Front Range areas; the Central Mountains, which includes the Vail, Summit County and Aspen areas; the Gunnison Valley, covering a large area from Crested Butte to Grand Mesa to Monarch Pass; and the San Juan Mountains. A map of each region at the beginning of each section will help you locate each center.

Legend for the Road Maps

+	Medical Center	━○━	Limited Access Highway
♠	U.S. Forest Service	──	Primary Highway
⋏	Scheduled Air Service	──	Secondary Highway
▄	Scheduled Bus Service	🄷🄾	U.S. Interstate
▰	Railroad Station	🄷🄷	U.S. Highway
┼─┼	Railroad Route	🄸🄸🄸	Colorado Route
▰	Car Rental	❸	County Route
·	Mountain Peak	🄳○	City, Town
⋉	Mountain Pass	⬭	Lake, Reservoir
⚘	Downhill Ski Area	⋯⋯⋯	Contintental Divide

Each region is then divided into sections which categorize the cross-country centers alphabetically under the headings of Touring Centers and Resorts; Ranches and Lodges; Miscellanea, which includes school programs, small ranches and trail systems; and Backcountry, which includes Guides, Hut Systems, Helicopter Skiing, and Backcountry Trails. Each cross-country center is viewed by: Trails, Rentals and Instruction, Accommodations, Guided Tours, Races and Special Events, Food and Lodging, and Access.

Generally, for each cross-country center described in the guide, a short history or description is given. Then a brief description of the trail system at each center begins with what can be called the "difficulty rating." This subjective rating system compares the trails at all the cross-country centers and gives them a classification relative to one another. It was developed to give the reader an idea of what type of skiing can be encountered at each center to allow him or her to make an informed decision as to which center would be best for his or her abilities. The ratings used are: easier, which describes trail systems that are the easiest to ski—flat tracks with easy turns; moderate, which describes the majority of trail systems, with more hills to climb and descend and trickier turns; and finally, more to most difficult, the hardest rating, which describes trail systems with the steepest hills, the highest elevations or the longest trails. Occasionally, trails at a cross-country center fall between two ratings, in which case the area is classed as easier-to-moderate or moderate-to-more-difficult.

Following the difficulty rating, the entire trail system is briefly described including the amount of trails maintained, how they are maintained, descriptions of the trail layout, and the center hours and fees. We have not attempted to describe all the trails at each cross-country center; the type of skiing encountered on each trail will vary according to the the amount of snow, weather and maintenance conditions at the time, and the ability of each skier using the trail.

In the Ranches and Lodges section, the accommodations offered at each area are described, and types of lodging, meal plans and the price of overnight stays are outlined.

Rentals and Instruction available at each cross-country center are then described, including the number and types of skis available to rent, the prices of the rentals, the type of instruction offered, the ability levels taught, instructive clinics offered, the number of instructors and their abilities or certifications, and the prices of the lessons.

Guided Tours are outlined next; this section covers tour destinations, the levels of ability appropriate for the tours, the types of tours offered, and the cost.

The Races and Special Events section briefly covers the races held at each center and mentions other events, such as cross-country presentations.

Food and Lodging, in the Touring Centers and Resorts section, are mentioned next, giving information to help you find accommodations and restaurants in close proximity to the center being described.

Finally, access to the cross-country center is explained, with directions to the area and the name and address of the person to contact for more detailed information. When you visit a cross-country center, be sure to let them know that you read about their operation in **Colorado Cross Country Skiing**.

In describing one cross-country center, we often refer to another. Some of the centers are connected to one another by trails, and clients are sometimes referred by one center to another for more appropriate service. When a center is mentioned by name, it is described somewhere in this book.

Trail Maps

The trail maps in this book will give you an idea of the extent and types of trails at each cross-country center. You may want to use them to compare the trails at each center before deciding which one to visit. The maps

Legend for the Trail Maps

=====	Road, Highway	☯	Easier Rating
——	Set Track	🝆	More Difficult Rating
‑ ‑ ‑ ‑	Packed Track	◇	Most Difficult Rating
— —	Backcountry Trail	🏠	Touring Center or Resort
•——•	Chairlift	🏘	Ranch or Lodge
USFS	U.S. Forest Service	🏠	Backcountry Hut

were compiled from each cross-country center's map; variations in scale and accuracy are to be expected. Miles/km scales were not available. Occasionally, we have omitted information we could not obtain, such as trail difficulty or name.

The symbols used on the trail maps to assign difficulty ratings for each trail are the standardized symbols adopted by the cross-country ski industry in this country. The symbols are relative to each area—an easier trail at one area may be a moderate trail at another—and in no way relate to our difficulty rating system used in this book.

Meal Plans

The standard meal plans offered at each ranch are mentioned in the Accommodations section under Ranches and Lodges. The meal plans are: the American Plan, which offers three meals a day included in the price of the room; the Modified American Plan, which includes two meals—breakfast and dinner—in the price of the room; and the European Plan, in which no meals are included in the basic room price.

Reservation Information

Where overnight stays are involved, each cross-country center has its own reservation, deposit and cancellation policy. We have not attempted to describe those policies in this book, but be aware that they exist.

Pricing

Prices listed in this book are 1985 prices and are subject to change. They were listed to give the reader an idea of what to expect at each cross-country center and to provide a comparison of one center to another. They are by no means to be considered as guaranteed prices. At some ranches and lodges, prices may vary according to the season—the Christmas season, for example, is the busiest one for many of the ranches, and some may raise prices during this time. Most prices listed do not include taxes or tips, which might be added to the cost of services.

Colorado Cross Country Ski Association

The Colorado Cross Country Ski Association (CCCSA) was developed in 1982 to promote cross-country skiing in Colorado as a fun, safe and healthy winter sport.

CCCSA has developed standardized definitions of maintained trails. These classifications have been used in this book. Machine-tracked or tracked trails are marked, mapped and signed for relative difficulty, they are regularly maintained, and the snow surface is groomed and/or tilled, after which ski tracks are set by machine. Packed trails are marked, mapped and signed for relative degree of difficulty, they are regularly maintained, the snow surface is compacted, and previous skiers' tracks may be present. Backcountry trails are marked or blazed, mapped, minimally maintained, the snow surface is seldom if ever groomed, and sign-out may be required or a starting time limit may be posted.

If a cross-country center is a member of CCCSA, it is mentioned in the center's section.

You can contact the CCCSA at P.O. Box 378, Granby, Co. 80446.

Professional Ski Instructors Association

The Professional Ski Instructors Association (PSIA), frequently mentioned in the Instruction section of each center, has developed standardized teaching methods for those interested in becoming ski instructors. PSIA-certified instruction assures the student of a proven, consistent approach to cross-country skiing.

Cross-country centers with instructors who are not certified by PSIA provide lessons based upon the experience of the instructors, and the quality of instruction can vary. Some instructors feel that their experience and teaching methods are superior to PSIA methods. If you are concerned with the quality of instruction offered at the center of your choice, check with that center for more information.

PSIA offers teaching clinics and examinations in various parts of the state and country to qualify a skier for certification as Associate Touring Instructor, Tour Leader Instructor, Advanced Instructor, Fully Certified Ski Touring Instructor, and Certified Mountain Ski Tour Guide classifications. PSIA will also certify ski schools according to standardized methods.

Interested people can contact PSIA-Rocky Mountain Division, P.O. Box 770004, Steamboat Springs, Co. 80477, (303) 879-8335.

Backcountry Trails

Colorado's backcountry provides the adventurous skier with rich rewards of spectacular scenery, solitude and challenge. Because of the enormous amount of National Forest land and fairly easy winter access, the state can boast a vast variety of backcountry ski tours.

The Backcountry Trails section provides a rough listing of local trails only. In a few cases these trails are closed to the public; always inquire locally before reaching a trail. We cannot assume responsibility for the condition and suitability of these trails.

Most trails and areas listed have a relative difficulty code: (E) is easier terrain for beginners, (M) is moderate for those of intermediate ability, and (D) is difficult, for experts only. (Where no code is given, difficulty information was unavailable.) The difficulty of a tour is subjective and depends on length and weather, so be conservative when considering your stamina and ability. Occasionally you will have to share the trail with snowmobiles. Access to trailheads may vary due to snow and weather; check ahead of time.

Terrain ranges from relatively flat meadows to rugged, dangerous high passes and peaks. Often a single trail can cross varied terrain. For safety, go with a guide or a friend who has skied that particular trail before; venturing into the backcountry alone is foolish. Select a tour that the least experienced member of your group can handle. Turn back when someone becomes too tired or cold. It is not worth the risk to go on even if you traveled hours to get to the trail.

As avalanches can occur nearly anywhere in Colorado, be sure to read the avalanche section in the Appendix.

The U.S. Forest Service

The Forest Service, generally the best basic source of information about the backcountry, is creating a large reference work called the Recreation Opportunity Guide (ROG) to catalog all of the outdoor activities in the National Forests. Most district offices have a large binder of information about their local areas. Cross-country skiing has its own section in the ROG; each trail has a brief review covering access, mileage and difficulty. Information on most of the trails and areas listed in **Colorado Cross-Country Skiing** has been taken from the Forest Service ROG. Check with the Forest Service for the condition of the trails and for avalanche danger before embarking on your tour; local ranger stations and their locations are listed at the end of the backcountry trail section.

Knowledgeable people at the cross-country centers and local ski stores can recommend trails to ski. The following are guidebooks about backcountry trails:

Northern Colorado Ski Tours, Tom and Sanse Suddulth, Touchstone Press 1976. 0-911518-44-4

Central Colorado Ski Tours, Tom and Sanse Suddulth, Pruett Publishing Co. 1977. 0-87108-518-6

50 Colorado Ski Tours, Richard DuMais, High Peak Publishing 1983.

There are, of course, more touring trails yet to be discovered (or reported). The lucky skiers are those who return to find their own special paths.

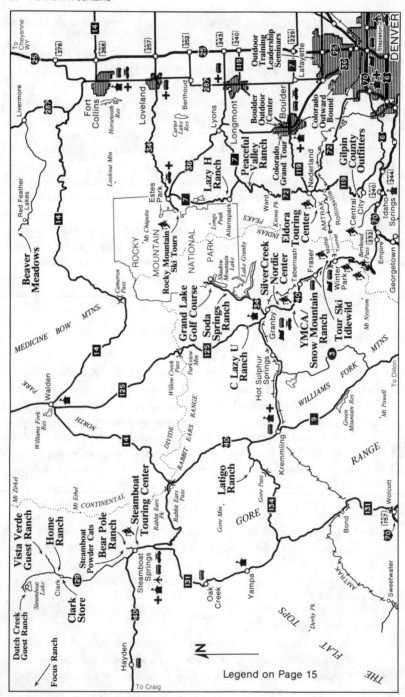

Legend on Page 15

Steamboat Springs Area

The cross-country centers discussed in this section are the Steamboat Touring Center and the Bear Pole Ranch located around Steamboat Springs, Home Ranch, Vista Verde Guest Ranch, Dutch Creek Guest Ranch, and the Clark Store situated farther north in and around the small town of Clark, and Focus Ranch located near Slater, close to the Wyoming border.

Steamboat Springs, in the Yampa Valley in northwestern Colorado, is bordered by the Routt National Forest. It sits west of the Park and Gore mountain ranges, and southwest of the Mount Zirkel Wilderness Area. Local industries include tourism, ranching in the Steamboat area, and coal mining to the south in Oak Creek. Visitors are attracted to Steamboat Lake, north of Steamboat Springs, for winter and summer seasonal recreation, to the downhill ski resort and hot springs in Steamboat Springs and the cross-country ski centers in the area.

Steamboat's skiing history dates back to the early 1900s when Marjorie Perry, a skiing enthusiast who skied from Steamboat Springs to Denver, introduced Carl Howelsen to the town. At that time, the potential for developing the sport at several areas in and around Steamboat Springs was great. Howelsen realized this potential by building the Howelsen Ski Jumping Complex in 1914 and planning the first winter carnival that same year. The carnival, the oldest in the state, continues every year. Howelsen Hill has been used for international ski jump competitions. The Steamboat downhill ski area on Mt. Werner opened in 1962. Sven Wiik, a cross-country skiing enthusiast, arrived in Steamboat Springs in 1968 and developed the sport of nordic skiing in the area.

Steamboat and Clark residents boast of the over 300 inches of "champagne" powder—light, fluffy, dry snow—that falls each year. The snow depth is locally described in terms of "wire winters"; this refers to whichever wire on a ranching fence is covered with snow. A three-wire winter is common; a four-wire winter is not uncommon.

Steamboat Springs is 157 miles northwest of Denver, with scheduled air service from Denver. If driving from Denver, take Interstate 70 to the Silverthorne-Dillon Colorado 9 Exit 205; follow Colorado 9 north to Kremmling and pick up U.S. 40 to Steamboat Springs. Continental Trailways bus also serves Steamboat.

Steamboat Touring Center

The Steamboat Touring Center, at 6,890 ft., was started in 1972 as part of the Steamboat downhill resort. In 1982, Sven Wiik was asked to run the touring center on the Sheraton Hotel's golf course and since then, nordic skiing's popularity has grown steadily each year.

The Wiiks are an active and interesting family. Sven, born in Sweden, was a ski instructor there until he moved to the United States in 1949. He began work in Gunnison as a ski coach and physical education teacher at Western State College, where he stayed for 19 years. During those years, he coached the nordic team of the Federation International de Ski, an international organization of skiers that holds world championships every four years, alternating with the Olympics. He was the nordic ski coach for the 1960 Olympics at Squaw Valley. In 1966 he was the university games coach in Italy for world competitions held between ski teams from international universities.

By August of 1968, Sven had moved to Steamboat Springs and begun construction on his Scandanavian Lodge, which he runs as a year-round resort today. He met his Danish wife, Birthe, in Sweden where she worked at a ski resort. They married and moved to the U.S. in 1954. Birthe is a potter and a weaver and plans the meals at the lodge.

The Wiiks' daughter, Birgitta, runs the touring center. On her first pair of skis at the age of two, she has ski touring in her blood and enjoys working in the same business as her parents'.

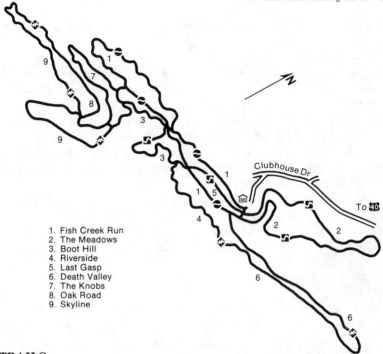

1. Fish Creek Run
2. The Meadows
3. Boot Hill
4. Riverside
5. Last Gasp
6. Death Valley
7. The Knobs
8. Oak Road
9. Skyline

TRAILS

The trails at Steamboat Touring Center are moderate in comparison to those of other touring centers mentioned in this book.

The 20 km of maintained trails meander through aspen and pine trees, travel up and down gentle hills, cross bridges over streams, and hardly seem to be part of a golf course. All trails are double-tracked and are groomed every day. Twenty-five percent of the trails are easier, 25% are intermediate and 50% are advanced trails. No warming huts are available, though the clubhouse at the head of the trails contains a ski and rental shop, a snack bar, and men's and women's locker rooms with showers. The snack bar serves lunches of homemade soups and breads as well as sandwiches and drinks. Sack lunches are available for full-day tourers.

Trail passes are $60 for the season if purchased before November 1, or $70 if purchased later. A family season pass for the first two members is $70 for each person; each additional member costs $35. The daily trail pass is $5, or $3.50 for children 12 and under. A five-day trail pass is $20 and a six-day trail pass costs $24.

RENTALS AND INSTRUCTION

Steamboat Touring Center has 110 pairs of Fischer skis to rent, including general touring skis, light touring skis, and racing skis, both waxable and waxless. Rentals for touring skis, boots and poles cost $6 for a half day or $7.25 for a full day.

Four full-time and three part-time instructors, all PSIA-certified, teach at Steamboat Touring Center. The school is a PSIA-certified ski school. Classes on basic track technique and on uphill and downhill skills are given twice a day. Scheduled times are 10 to 11:30 a.m. and 1:30 to 3 p.m. Private lessons are available.

All levels of instruction from introductory to beginning telemarking are given. Because of the terrain's gentle slopes, only beginning telemarking skills are taught. A telemark instructor is available at the Steamboat ski area if more advanced instruction is required.

Group lessons cost $15.75 per person. Private lessons are $21.75 per person and $12 for each additional person. A half-hour private lesson costs $12 per person. A full-day's lesson for children, including lunch, costs $29.75 per child; a half day costs $18.50 per child. Prices include a trail pass.

GUIDED TOURS

Guided tours are led up Rabbit Ears Pass. All-day tours, which last from 10 a.m. to 3:30 p.m., are the only tours available. These tours take place on National Forest land and can be arranged for all levels of ability. The trail is chosen according to weather conditions and the abilities of the individuals in each group. Alpine bowls on the pass make impromptu telemark lessons possible. Tours cost $18.75 per person and will take place only if at least five people have signed up by 10 minutes prior to departure time. Special-destination tours and private-party tours can be arranged and can run from 9:30 a.m. to 4 p.m. The cost is $100 for up to five people and $20 for each additional person.

RACES AND SPECIAL EVENTS

Steamboat Touring Center is involved with the community and actively encourages people to cross-country ski and race. Steamboat's first to fifth graders partake in lessons once a week for six weeks as part of a school program. The Citizens' Race Series involves a race every other Sunday for 10 Sundays. Everyone is encouraged to race; a minimum entry of six races is necessary for an individual to qualify for an award. The course varies for each race, although it is always 10 km in length. (Five kilometer and 3 km races are held for children and those who prefer the shorter race.) The Swix and Fischer companies are sponsors and donate awards. Other races include The Wood Ski Classic, a race for skiers with wooden skis, and a balloon race, which combines skiing with a 30-minute balloon ride.

The University of Wyoming holds NCAA qualifying races at the touring center, and the USSA-Rocky Mountain Division sponsors the Junior

Olympic qualifiers there in February. The Junior Olympic team, the Olympic team and the National Masters Championship team all practice there. Several clinics are held in November. One is the Instructor-Tour Leader School, referred to as a hiring clinic for skiers looking for a ski school position. A dealer's clinic, where ski equipment dealers are taught how to ski and to sell equipment, is held every year. At Thanksgiving, two clinics are available for those who wish to renew their skills and to learn new techniques. Also in November, PSIA holds a clinic for certifying new instructors.

FOOD AND LODGING

The snack bar located in the clubhouse serves lunches and sack lunches, as mentioned above. Additional restaurants and numerous overnight accommodations are available in both Steamboat Village (at the ski resort) and Steamboat Springs. For assistance in making reservations, call (303) 879-0740, or in Colorado, (800) 332-3204, or write Steamboat Chamber/Resort Association, P.O. Box 773377, Steamboat Springs, Co. 80477.

ACCESS

Take the Mt. Werner Road exit from U.S. 40, east of Steamboat Springs, turn left on Steamboat Blvd., turn right on Clubhouse Drive. Turn left to the golf course clubhouse and the ski center.

Contact Birgitta Wiik, Steamboat Touring Center, P.O. Box 774484-EEM, Steamboat Springs, Co. 80477, (303) 879-8180 or (303) 879-0517.

Bear Pole Ranch

Bear Pole Ranch is located only three miles outside Steamboat Springs. Once you are on the ranch, though, it does not seem possible that there is a town nearby. Views of the surrounding mountains and miles and miles of snow covered fields can be seen from anywhere on the ranch.

Bear Pole is run by Dr. Glenn and Rusty Poulter, owners of the ranch since 1966. Originally a place with special summer programs for children, it grew to include a winter ski ranch. The first program was a skiing camp for above-average skiers who had aspirations to become professionals.

In 1970, ski touring became a permanent addition. Though most of the guests remain downhill skiers, it is Dr. Poulter's hope that he may lure some of these people to the sport of cross-country skiing. The emphasis at the ranch is unquestionably nordic, with lessons and tours given daily.

A doctor of geology, Poulter has worked in South America, Africa, Canada and Europe. Rusty has a masters degree in guidance and counseling, has taught children in Venezuela and had her own day-care center in Steamboat Springs for years. The Poulters run a summer camp for children that features camping, backpacking and hiking in the United States and in Austria and Norway. They share obvious concern for and interest in both the guests and the staff at their ranch.

Bear Pole Ranch is a member of the Colorado Cross Country Ski Association.

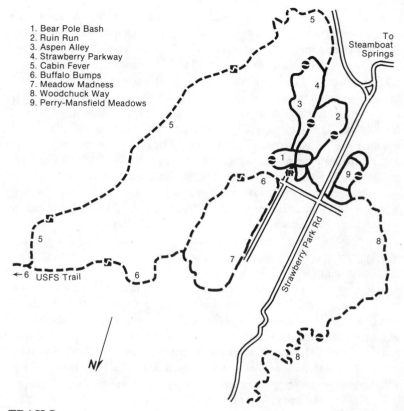

1. Bear Pole Bash
2. Ruin Run
3. Aspen Alley
4. Strawberry Parkway
5. Cabin Fever
6. Buffalo Bumps
7. Meadow Madness
8. Woodchuck Way
9. Perry-Mansfield Meadows

To Steamboat Springs

USFS Trail

Strawberry Park Rd

N

TRAILS

The trails at Bear Pole Ranch are rated easier to moderate in comparison to those of other touring centers mentioned in this book.

There are 10 km of machine-set trails, mostly beginner trails which meander over meadows and through aspen groves. Over 80 miles of trails are located nearby, including local trails and two backcountry trails accessible from the ranch. The "Buffalo Bumps" trail is a trail up Buffalo Pass Road which climbs 11 miles uphill and returns. These trails are not set but are packed or tracked by previous skiers.

The ranch also has access to a 12-passenger Thiokol Spryte snowcat, through the Steamboat Powder Cats, for transportation into the backcountry for high-country, powder skiing.

There is no charge to anyone for use of the trails at Bear Pole Ranch.

ACCOMMODATIONS

The lodge at Bear Pole houses a central dining room where diners are summoned by the ringing of a brass bell. Guests sit in front of a big fireplace at picnic tables set with candles and red tablecloths. The staff joins the guests at this friendly place where people get to know one another by first names and the conversation is lively. Breakfast and dinner are served buffet-style and guests are allowed all they can eat.

Visitors may stay in separate cabins, which accommodate six people in two sleeping rooms and a loft. Each cabin has a bath and fireplace. Dormitories, small cabins that sleep up to six people, share a nearby bathhouse. Large dormitory rooms sleeping 12-20 people share a common bath. A new building has fully carpeted family units with fireplaces and baths.

A rustic theme runs throughout the ranch—all the buildings are made of logs, the fireplaces of stone, and the furniture is handmade. Though rustic, the cabins are warm and comfortable.

Prices, which include lodging, breakfast and dinner, and transportation to and from Steamboat, range from $30 for dormitory rooms to $60 for a family unit. All prices are per person per night. Prices depend on the length of stay, the size of group and the season. Package plans for longer stays are also available.

Indoor evening activities include amateur hours and music by the fireplace; outdoor activities include snow tubing, with a fire and hot chocolate to warm you, or moonlight ski tours. The "barn," a large building used as a recreation hall, includes a volleyball net, ping-pong tables and enough room for a square dance. Guests are welcome to use these facilities at any time. Other activities available in the Steamboat area include ice fishing, sleigh rides, a ski jumping complex, ice skating, and downhill skiing.

Beware of the ranch's herd of pet rabbits!

RENTALS AND INSTRUCTION

A rental shop is located in the barn where 30 pairs of waxless touring skis are available, including some wooden skis. Rentals are priced at $4 for a half-day package; $6 a day for the one- to two-day package; and $5 a day for the three-day package.

At present there are six instructors at Bear Pole, aside from Dr. Poulter, all with considerable skiing and instructing experience. All levels of skiing are taught at the ranch, including telemarking; several gentle slopes test beginners' telemarking skills. A one-hour lesson costs $4.

GUIDED TOURS

A variety of guided tours are offered. A ski to the local hot springs pool, which is two miles one way, is made frequently. At times Dr. Poulter rents the hot springs pool for two hours for his guests. A moonlight meadow tour takes place right from your door when the moon is full. There are wine-and-cheese tours. Half-day and all-day tours are available up Rabbit Ears

Pass, where there are many backcountry trails. The price for an all-day tour with a guide is $8; a half-day tour with a guide costs $5; the hot-springs tour is $5; the moonlight-meadow tour is $4; and the moonlight wine-and-cheese tour is $6.

ACCESS

From Denver, take U.S. 40 through Steamboat Springs to 7th St., make a right and follow 7th until you reach Missouri St. Take Missouri, go several blocks to Park Ave. and turn left, following the sharp turns around Strawberry Park. Follow about two miles to a sign for Bear Pole Ranch on a telephone pole on the right, take that right and continue a half mile to the ranch. There is a shuttle available from the ranch to Steamboat Springs and the ski resort.

Contact Dr. and Mrs. Glenn Poulter, Bear Pole Ranch, Box-C, Star Route 1, Steamboat Springs, Co. 80487, (303) 879-0576.

Home Ranch

Ken and Sharon Jones moved from a ranch in Wyoming to Steamboat Springs in 1978 with a dream of building a working ranch and a cross-country ski touring center. It took them two years to build the ranch from the ground up on an exquisite site 20 miles north of Steamboat Springs. The ranch is at 7,300 ft. on 650 acres of meadows, aspen groves and hills. The views from the ranch include pastoral fields, Hahn's Peak, Sand Mountain and the Elk River valley. From many of the trails, the ranch's grazing herds of horses, cows, and llamas can be seen.

Home Ranch is a member of the Colorado Cross Country Ski Association.

TRAILS

The trails at Home Ranch are rated easier to moderate in comparison to those of other touring centers mentioned in this book.

Home Ranch has 26 km of well-laid-out trails on the ranch. Some trails stretch over meadows near the ranch, the cabins and the farm animals, and some climb up into aspen groves and onto an upper meadow where the views of the valley are unobstructed. The animals, especially the llamas, keep an eye on you to check your form and to be certain you are not sneaking any hay by them!

The terrain is covered with a full range of trails: 40% beginner, 40% intermediate and 20% advanced. Groomed often, most of the trails are single-tracked because there are so few skiers compared to the large number of

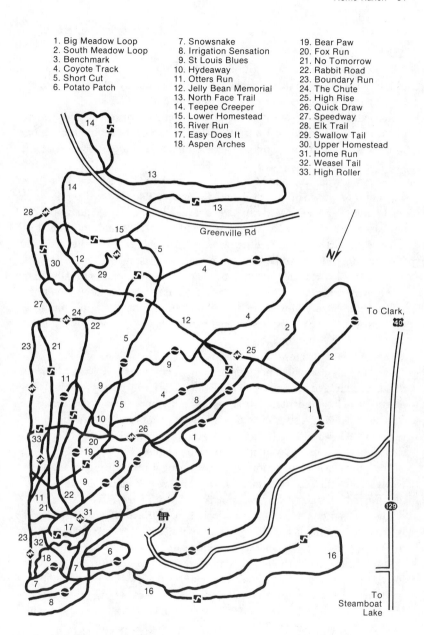

1. Big Meadow Loop
2. South Meadow Loop
3. Benchmark
4. Coyote Track
5. Short Cut
6. Potato Patch
7. Snowsnake
8. Irrigation Sensation
9. St Louis Blues
10. Hydeaway
11. Otters Run
12. Jelly Bean Memorial
13. North Face Trail
14. Teepee Creeper
15. Lower Homestead
16. River Run
17. Easy Does It
18. Aspen Arches
19. Bear Paw
20. Fox Run
21. No Tomorrow
22. Rabbit Road
23. Boundary Run
24. The Chute
25. High Rise
26. Quick Draw
27. Speedway
28. Elk Trail
29. Swallow Tail
30. Upper Homestead
31. Home Run
32. Weasel Tail
33. High Roller

trails. Several places on the ranch are perfect for practicing your telemark skills.

No fee is charged for the use of the trails.

ACCOMMODATIONS

The center of the ranch is an enormous lodge of log construction that contains the dining area, the ranch kitchen, a library, a children's playroom, a living room, a sun room and greenhouse, and the office.

The lodge is comfortable and tastefully designed. Large windows in many of the rooms add light and warmth. High ceilings with ceiling fans, rough wood walls, and antique and homemade furniture combine to make a special and homey atmosphere.

The guests, a maximum of 16 in winter, stay in their own cabins. Seven log cabins of varying sizes, each with its own outdoor hot tub, porch, small refrigerator and coffee-maker, are nestled in the aspen groves. Well-insulated and furnished with custom-made furniture and antiques, they have large, modern bathrooms. Most of the cabins have one bedroom, though some have two bedrooms and a living room.

Three meals a day are included in the package prices offered. Breakfast and lunch are served buffet-style and the sit-down dinner is served family-style, with serving bowls on the table. At every meal you are served all you can eat. The cooking has won so much praise that Ken has published a cookbook of ranch recipes.

One of the requirements for landing a job at Home Ranch is having the ability to play a musical instrument. The ranch boasts its own bluegrass band, which plays in town some weekends. The living room is partially furnished with instruments: a stand-up bass, a piano, guitars and an organ. The band can be persuaded to play in the evenings and guests are invited to join in. (Ken plays guitar and bass and writes songs; Sharon plays classical piano and will play before dinner on request.)

The ranch has a recreation room with a pool table, a ping-pong table, and a stereo and VCR system. VCR tapes are rented on request. Many people prefer to soak in their own hot tubs after a hard day of skiing.

Every afternoon at around 1 o'clock, a sled drawn by a team of horses is driven to the fields to feed the ranch animals. Guests are invited to join in the feeding or just go along for the ride.

A staff babysitter is available if needed. There are no specific programs for children, though there is a playroom stocked with toys.

Home Ranch caters to cross-country skiers and offers packages of three, four and seven nights, costing $295, $385, and $640, respectively, per person, double occupancy. The package prices include use of the trails, unlimited lessons, trail guides, equipment, three meals a day, maid service, hot tub and shuttle service to and from Steamboat Airport. Children's rates and lower prices for groups are available.

RENTALS AND INSTRUCTION

Home Ranch has 50 pairs of skis to rent, all waxless, touring skis. The rental shop is equipped for repairs or quick fixes. Mementos of Home Ranch—mugs, hats, pins, etc.—and a small selection of skiing necessities can be purchased.

All levels of skiing, from beginning to telemarking, are taught by three instructors. One instructor, the head of the program, is PSIA-certified, and the other two are working on their certifications. (Sharon is one of the instructors.) Telemarking is taught on a gentle slope perfect for learning the telemark position and turns.

Lessons are given at 9:30 a.m. daily, but can be given any time during the day by appointment.

GUIDED TOURS

Home Ranch recommends that guides be used whenever guests venture into the backcountry. Their guides are trained to help in emergency situations and are equipped with tools necessary in the event someone breaks a ski or loses a binding. Several guided tours are given from Home Ranch. One, a day trip up north, is about six miles round-trip to a cabin used by Home Ranch as a warming hut. Lunches are provided. Home Ranch has a snowcat that can transport people to an old ski hill for a day of telemarking in deep powder. Tours are also given in the surrounding Routt National Forest.

ACCESS

From Steamboat Springs, about one mile west on U.S. 40 at the stoplight, turn right onto County 129. Follow 18 miles to Clark, then a half mile past Clark to a sign on the right to Home Ranch. You can't see the ranch from the highway; it is about a half mile in.

Contact Ken and Sharon Jones, Home Ranch, P.O. Box 822-G, Clark, Co. 80428, (303) 879-1780.

Vista Verde Guest Ranch

Frank and Winton Brophy moved to their ranch in Clark in 1973 from Westchester County in New York, after deciding to start a family-centered business. The ranch began as a summer guest and working ranch where cattle and horses were raised. In 1979, the winter recreation program was added.

Vista Verde, at 7,800 ft., is situated on 508 acres outside Clark, 25 miles north of Steamboat Springs. It is surrounded by the Mt. Zirkel Wilderness area and Routt National Forest; trails in both areas are accessible on skis from the ranch. The ranch is bordered by the Elk River.

Vista Verde is a member of the Colorado Cross Country Ski Association.

TRAILS

The trails at Vista Verde are moderate in comparison to those of other touring centers mentioned in this book.

Twenty kilometers of trails are packed by snowmobile rather than tracked, though the staff will set track if requested by guests. The trails cross meadows and travel into the surrounding forests...40% of the trails are in the trees. The forest-protected trails, though maintained, are like backcountry trails; the Brophys like to say that their trails are for people who enjoy being surrounded by nature. Elk, deer, fox and coyote are occassionally spotted.

The trails cover from beginning to advanced terrain, and there are two telemark hills on the ranch covered with the powder Steamboat residents love to brag about.

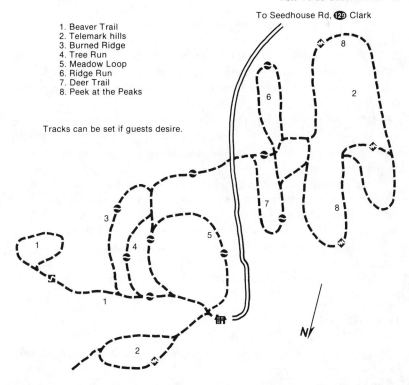

To Seedhouse Rd, **129** Clark

1. Beaver Trail
2. Telemark hills
3. Burned Ridge
4. Tree Run
5. Meadow Loop
6. Ridge Run
7. Deer Trail
8. Peek at the Peaks

Tracks can be set if guests desire.

There is no charge to overnight guests to ski the trails.

ACCOMMODATIONS

The ranch is composed of a main lodge and several cabins, four of which are open for guests in the winter. Each cabin holds about six people. The cabins are perched on an aspen-studded hillside and are built of spruce logs, with rough logs making the inside walls. Each is carpeted, has central heating, a living area, a small but fully equipped kitchen, a bathroom, and one to three bedrooms (some have lofts). Furnished with hand-built pine furniture, each has its own woodstove, and the supply of wood on each porch seems endless. Picture windows overlook the pastures and farm animals.

In the lodge, a big living area is filled with a large table and benches, comfortable chairs, and is heated by an efficient woodstove insert in a stone fireplace. Collections of pewter, glass bottles, and candlesticks, and a beautiful grandfather clock will attract your attention. A library downstairs holds plenty of books available for borrowing. Upstairs is a recreation room with games and a TV.

The Brophys plan to make a few additions and changes by 1986. A sauna and a jacuzzi will be built. In addition to the European Plan, the American Plan will be available starting the winter of 1985-86.

The Brophys are proud of the personal atmosphere at Vista Verde. Because there are so few guests at one time, they can give special attention to each person.

Sleigh rides, snowshoeing, slalom snowboarding, ice fishing (at Steamboat Lake), and downhill skiing (at Steamboat) are available. Although snowmobiling is discouraged on the ranch, there are snowmobile trails in the vicinity.

Taking a ride on the sled to feed the horses is an enjoyable diversion. The sled is pulled by two Belgian draft horses, Daisy and Diamond. You can hop on the sled and see how the horses are fed. Then you can try to keep track of the numerous farm cats, all ready for some attention.

The lodging-and-meals package costs $70 a day per person during the regular season. For the Christmas season, the charge is $100 a day per guest. Lodging without meals costs $85 a day per cabin in the regular season, or $120 per day per cabin during the Christmas season.

RENTALS AND INSTRUCTION

Rentals are not available at the ranch. Those who need equipment can rent it in Steamboat Springs or at the Clark Store. The Brophys will help make arrangements for you.

The Brophys and one other member of the staff teach beginner through telemark lessons; the instructors have all taken PSIA clinics at Steamboat Touring Center. Lessons cost $8 per person for a 1-1/2 hour group lesson, or $15 per person for private lessons.

GUIDED TOURS

Guided tours are given by the staff on National Forest trails. A network of these trails is accessible from the ranch. South Fork, following the South Fork of the Elk River, is a 15 km trail marked by the Forest Service; two other trails are Hinman Creek and Hole In The Wall Canyon. Fees for a half-day tour are $10 per person. An all-day tour costs $20 per person.

ACCESS

From one mile west of Steamboat Springs on U.S. 40, take County 129 for 18 miles to Clark. After Clark take the right fork onto Seedhouse Road. Follow for five miles to the left-hand driveway with the Vista Verde Guest Ranch sign over the road. The ranch is about a half mile down the driveway.

Contact Frank and Winton Brophy, Vista Verde Ranch, P.O. Box 465, Steamboat Springs, Co. 80477, (303) 879-3858.

Clark Store

The Clark Store, under new ownership in winter 1985, is developing a cross-country center, including maintained trails, lessons and rental equipment, right in the town of Clark. The town sits in the Elk River Valley and is surrounded by large ranches and rolling foothills. This general store supplies everything from skis to beans and flour, as well as rentals of cross-country equipment. A post office and liquor store are located in the same building.

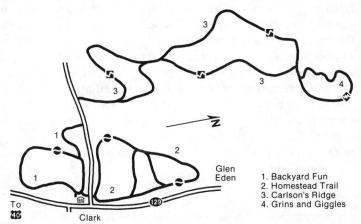

1. Backyard Fun
2. Homestead Trail
3. Carlson's Ridge
4. Grins and Giggles

The trails maintained by the Clark Store are rated easier in comparison to those of other touring centers mentioned in this book. The ski trails are groomed and tracked and lead from the store to wander through the neighboring hills and hay meadows. At least 15 km of trails are maintained.

The manager of the store, Brick Root, worked for years at a cross-country ranch in Montana. Root and two other staff members are experienced PSIA-certified instructors and are available for lessons and backcountry tours. All levels of ability can be accommodated.

One ski trail leads to nearby Glen Eden Lodge, where rooms and meals are available. Additional food and lodging is available in Steamboat Springs.

ACCESS

From Steamboat Springs on U.S. 40, about one mile west at the stoplight turn right onto County 129. Follow 18 miles to Clark; the store is on the left-hand side of the highway.

Contact Brick Root, The Clark Store X-C, P.O. Box 825, Clark, Co. 80428. (303) 879-3849.

Dutch Creek Guest Ranch

In the winter of 1985, Dutch Creek Guest Ranch opened for the first time. Located on a road not plowed until a few years ago, the 100-acre ranch is situated in a beautiful spot. Past Hahn's Peak settlement and overlooking Steamboat Lake, it is nestled in pine trees surrounded by Routt National Forest. Four newly built cabins are completely furnished and include a living room, a fully equipped kitchen, a modern bathroom and bedrooms. The cabins have sliding glass doors overlooking Hahn's Peak and Steamboat Lake. Each cabin holds six people; the ranch's total capacity is 24.

Glenda and Lawson Casad moved to Clark and built their ranch in 1984, leaving the hustle of the city behind to enjoy the quiet and seclusion of the country. As of this printing, the Casads weren't quite sure what path the ranch would take...they wanted to be open to the desires of the public. During the winter of 1985, they had packed ski trails around the ranch and into the surrounding forests. They hope to continue maintaining ski trails in the years ahead. A 10 km and 3 km cross-country ski race was sponsored in March of 1985 to encourage people to visit the Steamboat Lake and Dutch Creek areas in the winter.

The fees are $65 per cabin per night, with no seasonal differences. No meal plan is offered.

ACCESS

From one mile west of Steamboat Springs on U.S. 40, take County 129 north 18 miles to Clark. Past Clark, take the left-hand fork toward Steamboat Lake and Hahn's Peak Village. Follow for about eight miles past the fork and Steamboat Lake to a left-hand turn and a sign pointing toward Dutch Creek. One more mile brings you to Dutch Creek Guest Ranch.

Contact Lawson and Glenda Casad, Dutch Creek Guest Ranch, P.O. Box 846, Clark, Co. 80428, (303) 879-8519.

Focus Ranch

Focus Ranch is located near the upper end of the Little Snake River Valley, northwest of Steamboat Springs. Bounded on the north by the Medicine Bow National Forest, it is 15 miles from the Continental Divide and close to the Wyoming border.

The ranch buildings, a lodge and several cabins are of log construction. All the cabins have private baths. Three meals a day are served family-style in the ranch dining room in the lodge.

Focus Ranch is open to groups of cross-country skiers by reservation. Groups of 10 to 12 people are welcome and can work with Terry Reidy, the owner, to arrange the visit to each group's liking. No trails are tracked on the ranch. You can ski on the ranch property or in the backcountry, where trails can be packed by snowmobile before each tour if the group prefers. The surrounding countryside offers miles of skiing, and loops as long as 20 miles can be planned. Elk, mountain lion, coyote and eagles can occasionally be seen from the trails.

The ranch does not provide cross-country instruction, guided tours or equipment rentals.

Winter rates are $325 per person per week, with discount rates available for large groups. Prices include lodging, meals, use of the ranch facilities, and skiing trails.

ACCESS

From Colorado there is no direct access during the winter, though it is 52 miles from Steamboat Springs on County 129 in the summer. Access from Wyoming is from Baggs; take Wyoming 70 to Slater.

Contact Terry Reidy, Focus Ranch, Slater, Co. 81653, (303) 583-2410 for more detailed directions.

Steamboat Powder Cats

Steamboat Powder Cats is owned by Jupiter and Barbara Jones. Their two 12-passenger Thiokol Spryte snowcats transport skiers up Buffalo Pass to the Continental Divide in Routt National Forest. Since all skiing is done in untracked powder, intermediate to expert skills are necessary. Both nordic and alpine skiers are welcome. A qualified guide accompanies each group; each guide is an EMT. A group can ski 10 to 15 runs per day for approximately 10,000 vertical feet of downhill skiing.

Reservations are needed in advance. A limited amount of Research Dynamics alpine powder skis are available at no charge.

Skiers are picked up by the Bear Pole Ranch van at Gondola Square in Steamboat Springs at 7:30 a.m. and are taken to Bear Pole Ranch, where the snowcat departs for Buffalo Pass.

A day with the Steamboat Powder Cats includes transportation from Gondola Square, a continental breakfast and orientation meeting, transportation to the backcountry, a full day of guided skiing, lunch on the mountain, and transportation back to Steamboat. This is all included in the $105-per-day price.

Contact Jupiter and Barbara Jones, Steamboat Powder Cats, P.O. Box 2468, Steamboat Springs, Co. 80477, (303) 879-5188 or (303) 875-0576.

Backcountry Trails

Clark area: Hahns Peak Lake (EM); Hahns Peak (MD); Steamboat Lake State Park trails; and the Seedhouse Road area (MD).

Steamboat Springs area: Hot Springs (M); Buffalo Pass (MD); Elk Park (D).

Rabbit Ears Pass area: Walton Creek Loop (EM); West Summit Loop (MD); North Walton Creek (MD); Fish Hook Lake (MD); Rabbit Ears Peak (MD); Hogan Park (D); Divide Trail (D); Long Park (D).

The Hahns Peak Ranger District—Routt NF, 57 10th St, Steamboat Springs, 80477, 879-1870—administers the above (except Steamboat Lake State Park).

Walden area: Michigan Lakes Ditch (MD); West Cameron Pass area (also see Front Range region); Willow Creek Pass area (also see Granby region); Arapaho Lakes area; Colorado State Forest.

The North Park Ranger District—Routt NF, 612 5th St, Walden, 80480, 723-4707—administers the above (except the Colorado State Forest where a State Parks Pass is required).

Yampa area: Bear River (E); Lynx Pass (E).

The Yampa Ranger District—Routt NF, 300 Roselawn, Yampa, 80483, 638-4516, administers the above.

(E) Easier, (M) Moderate, (D) Difficult.

Granby Area

The cross-country centers covered in this section are Tour Ski Idlewild, located in the town of Winter Park; the YMCA/Snow Mountain Ranch and SilverCreek Nordic Center just outside the town of Granby, north of Winter Park; the Soda Springs Ranch and the Grand Lake Golf Course farther north, south of Grand Lake and on the edge of Rocky Mountain National Park; the C Lazy U Ranch, northwest of Granby; and Latigo Ranch, located near Kremmling, about 30 miles west of Granby.

To the north and east of this region lie Rocky Mountain National Park and the Roosevelt National Forest, and to the west the Arapaho National Forest. Mountain ranges surrounding Granby include the Never Summer Range to the north, the Indian Peaks to the east, and the Vasquez range to the south. This region is the location of a large water storage project which provides water to the east slope, drawn from Lake Granby. The Fraser Experimental Forest is located in the Roosevelt National Forest, and logging and ranching operations make up much of the local industry.

Winter Park, Mary Jane, Ski Idlewild and SilverCreek offer downhill skiing. This has been a mecca for Denver skiers since 1928 when the Moffat Tunnel, through the Front Range, provided rail access to the Winter Park area.

Devil's Thumb Ranch and Tour Ski Idlewild provided the area's first cross-country ski centers. Devil's Thumb, a premier cross-country ski ranch, built a strong following over several years of operation, but unfortunately, has been closed to cross-country skiing since the winter of 1983-84.

Five of the cross-country operations in Grand County have organized the Winter Start Series cross-country ski races to promote nordic skiing in their area. The series consists of five races held over a period of 10 days in early December at each of the five touring centers around the county. Refer to each specific touring center for more details on the individual races.

Continental Trailways serves Fraser, Winter Park, Granby and Kremmling. Amtrak serves Winter Park and Granby. The Granby area is about 80 miles northwest of Denver; take Interstate 70 to Exit 232 to U.S. 40. Follow U.S. 40 over Berthoud Pass to Granby.

See Map on Page 20

Grand Lake Golf Course Ski Touring Center

People were skiing on the Grand Lake Golf Course for years before it was set with cross-country tracks. In 1982, with the help of Grand Lake Metropolitan Recreation District, a program of regularly maintained trails was begun. In 1985, the trail system became part of the Grand Lake Cross Country Ski Center after being connected to Soda Springs Ranch by a 10 km trail following a ditch road between the two centers. Trail passes are exchangeable between the two. Plans are being made for a warming hut on the long trail between Soda Springs and Grand Lake.

The clubhouse at the golf course is used in the winter as a small restaurant and bar, serving sandwiches, soup and chili. A rental shop and a retail ski shop are located there.

Grand Lake Golf Course Ski Touring Center is a member of the Colorado Cross Country Ski Association.

TRAILS

Trails at Grand Lake are rated easier to moderate in comparison to those of other touring centers mentioned in this book.

Between 10 and 15 km of trails are maintained on the golf course. They are double-tracked beginner and intermediate trails, which not only follow the fairways of the golf course but also enter into surrounding forests of spruce and lodgepole pine. No telemarking or advanced terrain is available here. Since the golf course is bordered by private land, there is no access to backcountry skiing. Rocky Mountain National Park, with several backcountry trails, is located nearby.

The trail fee is $2 per day.

RENTALS AND INSTRUCTION

Twenty pairs of Jarvinen waxless touring skis, all with the Salomon Nordic System of boots and bindings, are available to rent. There are also 18 pairs of children's skis, boots and poles, purchased for the touring center by the local Independent Sportsmen Club, available to children at no charge.

All-day rentals for adults cost $7, rentals for two hours cost $5. Skis, boots, and poles can be rented separately.

Lessons are given by several local instructors and must be arranged in advance so the instructors can be notified. Lessons given at the golf course cover only beginning and intermediate skiing and cost $8 per person for the duration of the lesson.

Moonlight tours are available by prior arrangement. The price depends upon the tour and how many people participate.

A special program is held for children every Monday—children under the age of 12 can have lessons, rentals and track skiing free of charge. This coincides with a program at Soda Springs Ranch that holds a day of free skiing for women on Mondays.

RACES

Three races are held at Grand Lake each year in conjunction with Soda Springs. The first race, held in early December, is part of the Winter Start Series and is a sprint relay. The second race, in early January, is a 5 km and 10 km race. The third, the Soda Springs/Grand Lake 15 km race, is held in early February. The Grand Lake Touring Classic is an independent race held in early March.

FOOD AND LODGING

As previously mentioned, snacks are available at the clubhouse. Restaurants and hotels are located in Granby, 20 miles south on U.S. 34.

ACCESS

Take U.S. 34 from Granby and follow for 17 miles to the intersection to Grand Lake. Take the left fork to Rocky Mountain National Park, then a second left shortly thereafter, and follow the signs to the golf course.

Contact D.W. Schlosser, Grand Lake Golf Course Ski Touring Center, P.O. Box 590, Grand Lake, Co. 80447, (303) 627-3402.

1. Trail Ridge
2. Meadows Edge
3. Noli Temere
4. Knobby Knoll
5. Cruiser
6. Running River
7. Nystrom
8. 3 Forks
9. Ernie's
10. Mirkwood
11. Hobbit
12. Lonely Mountain
13. Smaug's
14. Moonlight
15. Bilbo's
16. Red Top
17. Never Summer

To Granby

To Grand Lake

SODA SPRINGS RANCH

10 km connector trail between Soda Springs and Grand Lake along Red Top Valley Ditch

GRAND LAKE GOLF COURSE

To Grand Lake

Soda Springs Ranch

Soda Springs Ranch, at 8,500 ft., is a condominium resort complete with a cross-country skiing program, a golf club and an athletic club. The cross-country touring center has its base at the large clubhouse, which contains a restaurant, a ski rental and retail shop, locker rooms, and a bar and lounge.

Soda Springs Ranch's ski touring program was begun in 1983 by Joe and Carol Morales, two avid and experienced skiers. Carol worked at nearby SilverCreek for several years and Joe ran the ski store at the now defunct Devil's Thumb Ranch. The Moraleses groom the trails, instruct skiers and run the store and the skiing program.

In 1985, Soda Springs' trails were connected along a ditch road to the Grand Lake Golf Course, making this the first place in Colorado to connect two touring centers. Thirty-five kilometers of groomed trails are available between the two centers. Trail passes are exchangeable.

Soda Springs Ranch is a member of the Colorado Cross Country Ski Association.

TRAILS

The trails at Soda Springs Ranch are rated easier to moderate in comparison to those of other touring centers mentioned in this book.

The Moraleses maintain their own 15 km of trails on Soda Springs Ranch, and about 5 more kilometers of the connecting trail between Soda Springs and Grand Lake. Every trail is double-tracked. They intentionally planned most of their trail system through timber so trails would stay fresh while protected from the wind and sun, and so maintenance would be easier. This also makes for pleasant skiing. The majority of the trails are beginner and intermediate, but there are some tricky hills calling for expert classification. The ditch road leading to Grand Lake is on a one-percent grade and is an intermediate 10 km ski. These trails offer good track skiing and can be used for long-distance training. The trails are well maintained and marked. The trail fee is $2.

There is some access to backcountry skiing, but those who wish to backcountry ski are usually encouraged to try the trails in Rocky Mountain National Park, which is 10 miles away.

RENTALS AND INSTRUCTION

Fifty pairs of Fischer skis with the Salomon Nordic System of boots and bindings are available to rent. The majority of these skis are waxless touring skis; some racing skis are also available. The ski shop includes a retail section and a shop for ski maintenance and repair. A full-day ski rental costs $7.

Instruction is given by the Moraleses. Carol is attending clinics to become certified by PSIA. All levels of cross-country skiing are taught, from beginning to advanced. Telemarking lessons can be limited by of the lack of appropriate terrain; in very snowy years, terrain for telemarking is more abundant.

Two track lessons are given daily at 10 a.m. and 1 p.m. Lessons cost $8 for 90 minutes of instruction.

A women's clinic given every Monday includes free instruction with classes offered twice each day. This is complemented by a free day of skiing for children at the Grand Lake Golf Course.

RACES AND SPECIAL EVENTS

Soda Springs Ranch holds several races each year, some in conjunction with Grand Lake. The first race is part of the Winter Start Series and is a sprint relay held in early December. The next event is the Soda Springs 5 and 10 km race held in early January. The Soda Springs/Grand Lake 15 km race is held in early February. The Soda Springs 5 and 10 km race is held at Soda Springs only in early March.

GUIDED TOURS

Moonlight or candlelight tours can be given on Soda Springs' trails when scheduled in advance. Skiers are escorted along candlelit trails to a bonfire where they drink hot spiced wine and cider and toast marshmallows. Ten or more people are needed for these tours to take place. The cost is $5 per person, or $7 per person with rentals.

FOOD AND LODGING

The Athletic Complex offers a weight-lifting room, a racquetball court, a jacuzzi, and tennis in the summer. A full-service restaurant upstairs in the clubhouse serves breakfast, lunch and dinner, with a special brunch on Sundays and an all-you-can-eat dinner buffet on Wednesday nights. There is also a comfortable bar and lounge.

Lodging is available at the Soda Springs Ranch condominiums. These condominiums are time-shared and several are available for rent during the winter. They are arranged in a hexagonal shape around a central jacuzzi. The condominiums are fully furnished and kitchens are fully equipped. One-bedroom "cottages" hold four people; two-bedroom "townhouses" hold up to eight people. The price range is $55 to $110 per night, depending on accommodations, occupancy and length of stay.

Additional accommodations and restaurants are available in Granby, 15 miles away.

ACCESS

Soda Springs Ranch is located about 15 miles north of Granby on U.S. 34, on the left side of the highway.

Contact Joe and Carol Morales, Soda Springs Ranch, 9921 U.S. 34, Grand Lake, Co. 80447, (303) 627-3486 or 629-0512.

SilverCreek Nordic Center

The SilverCreek Nordic Center, at 8,220 ft., is part of a downhill skiing complex just outside Granby. A relatively young ski area, SilverCreek was opened in 1982. The nordic center has been part of the resort since 1983 and operates from a shop in the Sterling Center Base Lodge at the base of the ski lifts.

Kim Long, the director, has run the nordic program since its beginning and prides himself on the condition of the trails. His goal is to maintain high-quality tracks at all times and to encourage more skiers and racers to use them.

SilverCreek Nordic Center is a member of the Colorado Cross Country Ski Association.

TRAILS

The trails at SilverCreek are rated easier in comparison to those of other touring centers mentioned in this book.

Twenty-five kilometers of trails are maintained at this touring center, where skiers take lifts to get to the ski trails. The easier trails are a short ride up the Milestone lift or the Poma, and the more advanced trails are at the end of the Expedition lift. Beginner trails are maintained, on what were originally planned as development roads, on flat and rolling meadows, and are suitable for race training.

The upper trails have been made on old logging roads and follow a ridge between two peaks. Some of the descents from the ridge can be tricky as

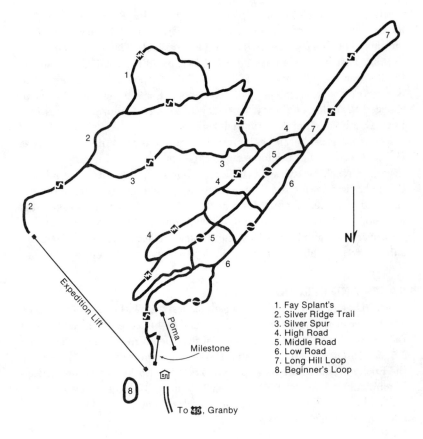

1. Fay Splant's
2. Silver Ridge Trail
3. Silver Spur
4. High Road
5. Middle Road
6. Low Road
7. Long Hill Loop
8. Beginner's Loop

is illustrated by the name of one of the trails—Fay Splants (read this fast!). Near the top of the SilverRidge trail is a nice view of the Fraser River Canyon.

The trails are 25% beginner, 60% intermediate and 15% advanced. They are all double-tracked, well-groomed and very pleasant to ski.

There is excellent telemarking terrain at SilverCreek; the downhill ski slopes are available for telemarking as well.

Track fees are $4 for adults for a full day and include two rides on the Milestone lift and Poma or one ride on the Expedition lift. Children 13 and under cost $3 for a full day. Half-day fees are $3 for adults and $2 for children; senior citizens over 60 may ski for free. Ten percent discounts are given for groups of 10 or more. Season passes are available. Women may ski free of charge on Thursdays. Operating hours are 9 a.m. to 4 p.m.

RENTALS AND INSTRUCTION

SilverCreek carries over 50 pairs of Fischer skis, all with Salomon Nordic System boots and bindings. The majority of the skis are waxless touring skis, though a few telemarking skis are available. The trail fee and rental package cost $11 for adults for a full day, or $8 for a half day. The cost for children 13 and under is $8 for a full day, or $6 for a half day. There is a 10% discount for groups of 10 or more. For rentals only, adults are charged $7.50 for a full day, or $5 for a half day. Children's prices for a full day are $5.50, or $3 for a half day.

Two instructors teach beginning through telemark skiing; one is certified with PSIA and both have much experience in teaching cross-country skiing. A teaching track by the lodge allows beginners to take a lesson before having to ride the lifts. Lesson fees, including one 90-minute session and track fee, are $12 for adults; $8 for children 13 and under; $25 for a family with a maximum of five people plus $5 for each additional student over the maximum. A three-hour telemark lesson costs $22 including a lift ticket, and a 1-1/2 hour telemark lesson is $15 without a lift ticket.

RACES AND SPECIAL EVENTS

SilverCreek has a busy race schedule, starting with one of the Winter Start Series races. This race is a 5, 10, and 20 km race and is held in mid-December. There is a 10 km and Biathlon Demo race in late December; a 5 and 10 km race and the SilverRidge (top-to-bottom) race in January; the Rocky Mountain Wanderers Volks Ski, the Rocky Mountain Masters Championships, and the SilverCreek 12 km run/12 km ski race in February; and the SilverCreek 10 km and Couples Finals and a Citizens' Biathlon and 10 km race in March.

FOOD AND LODGING

Lodging is available nearby in condominums at the ski area, or in a new 342-room resort hotel and conference center a mile from the ski area. Studio rooms to master suites are available; most are furnished with wet bars and refrigerators, personal whirlpool baths and steam cabinets. Room rates vary from $34.50 to $95 per night, depending on the length of stay and occupancy. There is no charge for children under two when with their parents. Two free tickets for either downhill or nordic skiing are given away per day per room.

There is a choice of three restaurants at this hotel, ranging from the black-tie Remington Room, serving gourmet dinners, to the Sunlight Cafe, serving lighter breakfasts, lunches and dinners, to the East Concourse, a deli offering sandwiches and soups.

Also located at the hotel are an athletic club with saunas, spas, steam rooms, and tanning salons; a pool; racquetball courts; two lounges; a large convention center; and gift, wine and flower shops.

Additional accommodations and restaurants are available in nearby Granby, or in Winter Park, about 15 miles away.

Childcare is available at the downhill resort for children from three months to seven years of age; for children from three to 12 months, 24-hour notice is necessary. The full-day charge for children is $16, two to four hours is $9, one to two hours is $3. A lunch and nursery school package is available at an additional cost.

ACCESS

SilverCreek is located three miles south of Granby and 15 miles north of Winter Park on U.S. 40. U.S. 40 is accessible from Interstate 70 at Exit 232.

Contact Kim Long, SilverCreek Nordic Center, P.O. Box 4001, Silver-Creek, Co. 80446, (303) 887-3384.

Tour Ski Idlewild

Tour Ski Idlewild, part of the Ski Idlewild resort, is one of the most well-established and popular cross-country touring centers in Colorado. The 40-year-old resort, located in the middle of Winter Park, consists of the touring center, an alpine ski hill with a lift, and a hotel and restaurant. The touring center became part of the resort in the winter of 1974-75. It is the oldest touring center in Grand County and has a reputation for being the best place in the county to learn telemarking.

TRAILS

The trails at Tour Ski Idlewild are moderate in comparison to those of other touring centers mentioned in this book.

Tour Ski Idlewild maintains 30 km of trails and, depending on the terrain, some are double-tracked, some single-tracked. The trails are divided evenly into beginner, intermediate and advanced trails. The trails are generally tracked through forests; many of them are narrow and winding and some have sharp curves at the bottom of hills.

No access to backcountry is available; those who are interested will find many backcountry trails at the top of Berthoud Pass, about 10 miles away.

The 800 ft. alpine hill at the resort is used for teaching and practicing telemarking. The touring center has its own building, which is a combination of a ski rental shop and a warming hut complete with hot drinks and reading material.

The trail fee is $3 for adults; there is no charge for children.

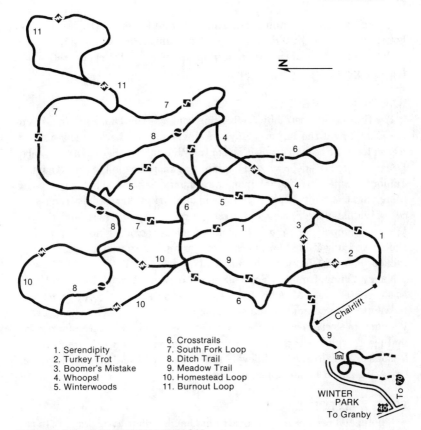

1. Serendipity
2. Turkey Trot
3. Boomer's Mistake
4. Whoops!
5. Winterwoods

6. Crosstrails
7. South Fork Loop
8. Ditch Trail
9. Meadow Trail
10. Homestead Loop
11. Burnout Loop

RENTALS AND INSTRUCTION

Tour Ski Idlewild has 115 pairs of Karhu skis, both waxless touring skis and telemarking skis, available to rent. Children of any age can be outfitted. The charge for adults is $10 and for children $7 for full-day rentals.

The teaching staff is composed of six full-time and part-time instructors. All the instructors are taught by Bill Howell, one of the managers of the center, who believes that the most effective way for people to learn to ski is on their skis out on the trails. The beginner's lesson starts on a flat area and progresses to an ideal trail for beginners—flat at first with a few small hills for learning uphill and downhill skiing techniques.

All levels of skiing, from beginning to advanced and including racing and telemarking, are taught. Many of the touring centers in the area send interested skiers to this resort for telemark lessons because of its reputation and its fine instructors and facilities.

A women's clinic is offered each year early in the season. It includes three days of lessons and touring.

A half-day group lesson costs $10; a private lesson is $18 for the first hour plus $12 for each additional hour. The telemark lesson, for $15, includes a lift ticket and use of the lifts following the lesson. Lift tickets costs $1.50 for a single ride.

RACES AND SPECIAL EVENTS

The first event hosted by the touring center is the Thanksgiving Training Camp, held the last few days of November or the first few days in December. The second event is one of the Winter Start Series races in early December, a citizens' race and a qualifying race for the U.S. Ski Team. A Junior Olympic Qualifier is run in late January. Scheduled in February and March are the Winterthon, an 8 km run and 12 km ski race between teams or individuals; the Spring Fling race, a point-to-point race; and the Ski Meister Competition, a low-competition event including nordic jumping, slalom and downhill skiing at Winter Park ski area, and a cross-country race at Tour Ski Idlewild.

Nancy Young, from the YMCA/Snow Mountain Ranch, teaches children at the center every Monday for the Bill Koch League, a group sponsored by World Cup champion and Olympic medalist Bill Koch, to encourage youngsters to cross-country ski. This instruction is conducted for a minimal fee charged at the beginning of the season, after which, rentals and lessons are free. Tour Ski Idlewild also helps outfit and gives trail passes to various local handicapped groups.

FOOD AND LODGING

A hotel and restaurant are located at the Ski Idlewild resort next to the touring center. A variety of accommodations and restaurants are available in the town of Winter Park, 1/8 of a mile away.

ACCESS

Winter Park is about 70 miles from Denver. Follow Interstate 70 to Exit 232 and take U.S. 40 over Berthoud Pass. U.S. 40 continues through Winter Park; look for a sign in the middle of town for the Ski Idlewild ski area. Buses serve Granby, and Amtrak serves both Winter Park and Granby.

Contact Bill Howell or Hugh Auchincloss, Tour Ski Idlewild, P.O. Box 1364, Winter Park, Co. 80482, (303) 726-5564 or (303) 887-2806.

YMCA/Snow Mountain Ranch

YMCA/Snow Mountain Ranch, at 8,700 ft., is located on 4,300 acres between Granby and Winter Park. Though the YMCA has been located at Snow Mountain Ranch since 1969 and people had been skiing there for years, it wasn't until 1982 that the potential of the ranch as a cross-country skiing haven was realized. In 1982 trail maintenance began, and in the winter of 1984 cross-country skiing on the ranch was eagerly promoted. Starting in 1986, old snowmobile trails will be converted into cross-country skiing trails, increasing the amount of maintained trails to 50 km.

Nancy Young has been the director of the nordic program since November of 1983. She is a Level II United States Ski Coaches Association (USSCA) coach and an associate coach of the U.S. Ski team.

Snow Mountain Ranch is a member of the Colorado Cross Country Ski Association.

TRAILS

The trails at Snow Mountain Ranch are moderate in comparison to those of other touring centers mentioned in this book.

Fifty kilometers of trails are maintained: 30% of the trails are beginner, 40% are intermediate, and 30% are advanced. They are all double-tracked with more tracks maintained in high-use areas. Trails cross over meadows into the surrounding forests and overlook the Front Range of the Rockies. Many of the trails are maintained for scheduled races and practices. Picnic tables are located on some of the trails.

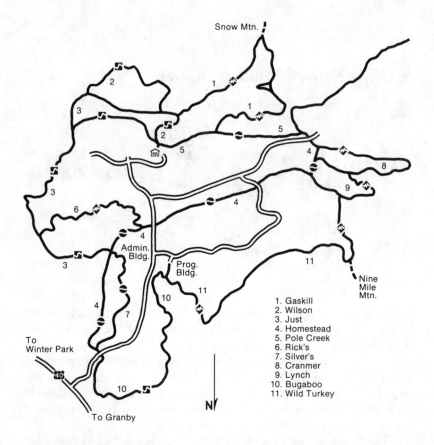

Snow Mtn.

2
3
2
5
1
1
5
4
8
9
6
4
3
Admin.
Bldg.
3
Prog.
Bldg.
4
11
4
7
10
11
Nine
Mile
Mtn.

To
Winter Park

10

To Granby

N

1. Gaskill
2. Wilson
3. Just
4. Homestead
5. Pole Creek
6. Rick's
7. Silver's
8. Cranmer
9. Lynch
10. Bugaboo
11. Wild Turkey

Most trails begin from the touring center at Camp Chief Ouray Dining Hall, which includes a rental shop, restrooms, tables, soda machine, fireplace, and a waxing area. In the winter of 1986, lunches will be served in the cafeteria above the touring center. Two other trails pass the Program Building, where skiers can find warm drinks and restrooms.

There is access to 15 km of backcountry trails from the ranch. People looking for backcountry skiing can ski to Blue Ridge and Nine Mile Mountain and to the top of Snow Mountain. Although there is no trail fee for these backcountry trails, Young asks that skiers sign in and out at the center as a safety precaution. There are no shelters located on these trails.

The trail fee is included with rentals or lessons. The trail fee for YMCA members is $2; children 12 and under pay $1; all others pay $4. Hours are 9 a.m. to 4 p.m. daily, early November to mid-April. Skiers are asked to register at the touring center with a route plan and return times.

RENTALS AND INSTRUCTION

YMCA has 150 pairs of Rossignol waxless and waxable skis with Salomon Nordic System boots and bindings. Skiers three years old and up can be outfitted. Also available are racing skis, high-performance touring skis and some telemark skis.

All-day rentals are $9; each additional day is $7; half-day rentals cost $5; children's skis are $3.50; group rates for eight or more are $4.50 each; senior citizens receive a discount of 50%.

Two instructors, both certified with the USSCA, teach all levels of skiing from beginning through racing. Their approach is to stress fitness in addition to correct skiing technique. Group lessons are $10 per person for a maximum of six people; private lessons are $20 plus $10 for each additional person.

People wishing to learn telemark skiing are sent to Tour Ski Idlewild, which has an ideal alpine hill and good telemark instructors. There is some appropriate terrain on Snow Mountain Ranch for practicing telemarking.

Young works with the Bill Koch League, a non-profit organization, offering skiing lessons to children. On Sundays, children from the Denver area are taught to ski at Snow Mountain Ranch, and on Mondays Young teaches local children at Tour Ski Idlewild.

Flanagan's, the largest alpine ski rental store in the area, offers equipment rentals and passes to the local ski resorts—Winter Park, Mary Jane and SilverCreek. A shuttle, called the Ski Lift, carries skiers to their skiing destinations.

ACCOMMODATIONS

Snow Mountain Ranch offers a variety of overnight facilities, including 45 cabins, four lodges and dormitory-type rooms. Each housekeeping cabin has two to five bedrooms and a kitchen, and is furnished with linens and cooking utensils. Two lodges, Aspenbrook and Silver Sage, have rooms with full baths, two double beds and a single bed. The Pinewood Lodge rooms have full baths, one double bed and two single beds. The Blue Ridge rooms have half baths, bunk beds and central showers. Dormitory rooms and youth camp lodges have bunk beds, central baths and showers.

The rates range from $20 per room to $110 per cabin, depending on the type of accommodation, occupancy and length of stay.

Meals are served in the Aspen Dining Room. There are restaurant and cafeteria facilities at the ranch. If the Modified American Plan is desired, add $12 a day to room rates for adults and $6 for children.

Other facilities at the ranch include an indoor swimming pool, a whirlpool, an Arts and Crafts Center, a gymnasium with a half-basketball court and a volleyball area, a roller rink, an ice-skating area, conference facilities, a gift shop, a snack bar, a grocery store, a laundromat, a gas station and a chapel. Rental equipment is available.

Babysitters are available, for children under three years old, on advance notice. There is a youth program for children over three years which includes a number of activities, such as swimming, ice skating, skiing, and roller skating. The charge for youth program is $10 a day per child three years old and over.

RACES AND SPECIAL EVENTS

The first race of the year is a mass-start 10 km race, part of the Winter Start Series held in early December. This is a citizens' race as well as a qualifying race for the U.S. Ski Team. The Snow Mountain Stampede, held every January, is the first race of the Great American Ski Chase, a series of eight races held at different sites throughout the United States. This event includes a 25 km ski race and a 50 km marathon race.

The Governor's Cup race, sponsored by the governor, is part of a series of yearly events taking place around Colorado to promote fitness and health. The series includes a cross-country ski race, a bicycle race, a running race and a triathlon. The cross-country race is a 10 km event and people of all ages are invited to participate. The governor himself participates. This race, in February, will take place at the Snow Mountain Ranch in 1986 and 1987.

Also held at the ranch are qualifying races for the Junior Olympics, the Special Olympics, a Level I USSCA Clinic, a USSCA Women's Clinic, and a Rossignol Demo Day.

Snow Mountain Ranch works with handicapped groups and their counselors to set up a skiing program tailored to each group's needs. They will outfit each person and assist counselors in teaching their groups to ski.

ACCESS

From Denver, take Interstate 70 to Exit 232, U.S. 40. Take U.S. 40 north over Berthoud Pass. Snow Mountain Ranch is located seven miles south of Granby on U.S. 40. Continental Trailways Bus serves Granby and Amtrack serves Winter Park and Granby.

Contact Nancy Young, YMCA/Snow Mountain Ranch, P.O. Box 558-EE, Granby, Co. 80446, (303) 887-2152.

C Lazy U Ranch

C Lazy U Ranch is one of Colorado's oldest guest ranches, and for the last six years has won the Mobil Travel Guide's Five-Star Award as one of the top resorts in the country. It has also received Triple A's Five-Diamond Award for five consecutive years. This luxurious ranch is well-known for its gourmet meals. Situated outside Granby, at 8,200 ft., it can accommodate more than 100 guests in the summer and handles an average of 40 guests during the winter.

Randy George and John Fisher direct the ranch's cross-country ski program. Both are the co-founders of the Colorado Cross Country Ski Association of which the ranch is a member.

TRAILS

The trails at C Lazy U Ranch are moderate in comparison to those of other touring centers mentioned in this book.

The 40 km of maintained trails are all double-tracked by state-of-the-art equipment. Instructors boast that they have the best trails in the state. One trail in particular, the Logging Trail, is the ranch's favorite. An intermediate 10 km trail, it affords a 180-degree view of the surrounding mountains and is accessible to beginners; it is rated intermediate only because of its length. Instructors are enthusiastic about teaching beginners on this particular trail—it affords skiing beginners can handle together with spectacular views normally accessible only to more advanced skiers. A trail such as this may encourage beginners to do more track and backcountry skiing.

1. Mesa Trail
2. Meadow
3. McQueeries
4. Logging Trail
5. Spring Trail
6. Peak-A-Boo
7. Wilson
8. Baldy

To Walden

To 40, Granby

The remainder of the trails are about 30% beginner, 60% intermediate and 10% expert. Backcountry trails on both private ranch land and National Forest land offer expert runs to advanced skiers.

ACCOMMODATIONS

Situated on 2,000 acres, C Lazy U Ranch raises 150 horses for riding programs in the summer. The main lodge, built in the 1950s of pine logs and beams, has a large lounge, a beautiful dining room, a well-stocked bar, and a small meeting or card room. All the rooms are decorated in a western motif complemented by Indian art. It is in the lodge that people gather for socializing and for all their meals.

Guests stay in a variety of accommodations. Small private rooms attached to the lodge are furnished with twin or double beds. Some of the rooms are connected to make suites; several other buildings contain suites of two bedrooms and two bathrooms for larger groups or families. One lodge has smaller suites. Several rooms have fireplaces; all rooms are warm, carpeted, roomy and comfortable. None have phones or televisions. Fresh fruit is provided in each room every day.

A large recreation hall has room for dancing, a ski rental shop, a whirlpool and sauna, two lounges, a conference room, and a game room with pool, ping-pong, and foosball tables.

The food served at the ranch is a story in itself. Three meals a day are included in the price of each room. Breakfast is served both buffet-style and restaurant-style. The buffet offers freshly-squeezed orange juice, homemade Danish pastry and rolls, and homemade granola and assorted cereals. Guests may also order anything from scrambled eggs to buttermilk pancakes. Lunch and dinner are single entrees only, served with homemade soups, salads with homemade dressings, homemade breads and fresh fruit. Desserts are homemade, of course; the challenge is to find room for them!

Rates include room and meals, use of the cross-country trails and equipment, skiing instruction, racquetball, horse-drawn sleigh rides, ice skating (rentals are available), sledding (C Lazy U holds high-speed sled races down their driveway), snow-tubing, sauna and whirlpool, and supervision of children during the Christmas holidays. Shuttle service is provided to several alpine resorts located in Granby and Winter Park. Laundry facilities are available. Prices range from $75 to $150 per person per night, depending on occupancy and season.

Although there is no specific childcare program, an instructor will supervise children's skiing and other activities.

RENTALS, INSTRUCTION AND GUIDED TOURS

The ranch has 40 pairs of Trak skis, mostly waxless light touring skis, to lend to guests.

There are three full-time instructors. All levels of skiing, from beginning to telemarking, are taught. Telemarking is quite popular and there are several practice areas.

Guided tours and moonlight tours are led on the trails and in the backcountry—these are included in the nightly rate. A special biathlon, held occasionally, features skiing and shooting balloons with pellet guns.

ACCESS

C Lazy U Ranch provides courtesy pick-up at the Amtrak station in Granby and the Continental Trailways bus station in Winter Park. If driving, take Interstate 70 from Denver to Exit 232. Take U.S. 40 and follow to Colorado 125, three miles west of Granby. Follow Colorado 125 3-1/2 miles and turn right at the C Lazy U gate.

Contact Randy George, C Lazy U Ranch, P.O. Box 378, Granby, Co. 80446, (303) 887-3344.

Latigo Ranch

Latigo Ranch is owned and run by Bill and Carol Hillier and their three children. Set on 1,700 acres outside Kremmling, the ranch has been run as a guest ranch since 1982. A cross-country skiing program was added in 1983-84. "Latigo" is the term used for a leather strap which adjusts saddle girth.

During the winter of 1984-85, the ranch was closed for improvements and expansion, so the cross-country ski program is still fairly new. The Hilliers, admitted novices to cross-country skiing, have oriented their trails for beginners and intermediates.

One of the improvements made during the winter of 1985 was a new road to the ranch. The Forest Service also plans to improve the road that leads to the ranch driveway, making the access easier.

Latigo Ranch is a member of the Colorado Cross Country Ski Association.

TRAILS

Trails at Latigo Ranch are rated easier in comparison to those of other touring centers mentioned in this book.

The Hilliers maintain 20 km of trails on their meadows and through the neighboring National Forest. Up a nearby ridge is a 3,000-acre meadow perfect for touring.

Though trails are generally for beginners, a full range of skiing terrain is available, including a packed hill for learning and practicing telemark-

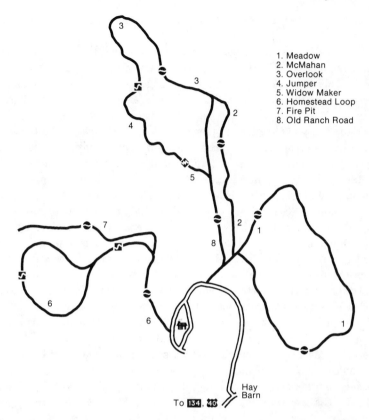

1. Meadow
2. McMahan
3. Overlook
4. Jumper
5. Widow Maker
6. Homestead Loop
7. Fire Pit
8. Old Ranch Road

ing. Some skiing is done on the ranch's summer horse trails, which are old logging roads and are maintained for skiers.

The trails have sweeping views of the Front Range; the Hilliers say that their ranch excels in views and silence. Access to National Forest land is possible from the ranch and most of the skiing is through timber.

Day visitors are encouraged to use the trails and are charged a $4 trail fee. Those who purchase a trail pass can use the ranch facilities for rentals, instruction, and lunch. Trails are free for overnight guests. Though there are no snowmobile trails on the ranch, a nearby backcountry trail leads to Rabbit Ears Pass near Steamboat Springs. There are no snowmobile rentals, but snowmobilers are welcome to use the ranch's facilities.

ACCOMMODATIONS

Guests stay in one of 10 cabins. Four of these are one bedroom cabins, built in a fourplex, each with its own porch and fireplace. Three back-to-back duplexes are three-bedroom cabins with private porches and fireplaces.

All cabins have electric heat and are a short walk from the center of the ranch.

Since the renovation, the original lodge is now used as the dining area and home for the Hilliers. Dining takes place in three separate rooms at wooden tables with handmade chairs. All the rooms have lovely views of the ranch and the mountains. Ranch-style meals are served three times a day.

The capacity at the ranch is 45 people, the average 30. The Hilliers like it that way, so they can enjoy getting to know each guest personally. Carol says, "These guest ranches are built around families, so each one reflects the family within. We are interested in a down-home family setting and in young adults, and it shows in the way we run our ranch."

A brand new "Social Club" was built in 1985 to accompany the older lodge. The club, built entirely of wood cut from the surrounding area, is rich and warm. The ground floor consists of a game room, a weight room, a hot tub, meeting facilities for 50 to 60 people, and a player piano with stacks of music rolls. The second floor has a two-story cathedral ceiling with ceiling fans and western-style chandeliers. This room, furnished with leather couches and chairs, has a huge stone fireplace and an enormous dance floor for square dances in the summer. (Dances can also be arranged in the winter if guests so desire.) There is also a lounge on the second floor. The upper level is a loft-library with a substantial amount of books.

Activities at the ranch include night skiing, horse-drawn sleigh rides, ice skating, snowshoeing, music in the lounge, videos, and movies. Four down-hill ski areas are within 40 miles of the ranch. There are no specific programs during the winter for children. Christmas is an old-fashioned one where the guests are encouraged to participate in decorating the ranch, baking cookies, and making their own ornaments.

The nightly rate of $64 per person for adults includes cabins, meals, all instruction, and use of the trails and equipment. The charge for children is $50 per night. There is a minimum of three days' and two nights' stay.

RENTALS, INSTRUCTION AND GUIDED TOURS

The ranch has 80 pairs of Elan skis, all waxless and general touring models, to lend overnight guests and rent to day visitors.

One instructor from Kremmling, an endurance skier, is certified with PSIA and is hired to teach all levels of skiing from beginning to telemarking. He is willing to teach guests whenever they are in the mood to learn.

Rentals and instruction are included in the nightly rates.

There are no guided tours as of this writing, though upon request, the instructor will give on-the-trail instruction and tour with skiers. Plans for the future include guided day tours into the surrounding National Forest.

ACCESS

From Interstate 70, take Exit 205 to Colorado 9 north to Kremmling. Pick up U.S. 40 north and follow for six miles to Colorado 134. Follow Colorado 134 for approximately two miles and take the first right-hand turn possible, on Red Dirt Road, between two ranch houses. Follow this for eight miles, taking right forks when possible.

Contact Bill and Carol Hillier, Latigo Ranch, P.O. Box 237, Kremmling, Co. 80459, (303) 724-3596.

Joe Morales at Soda Springs Ranch waxing skis.

Backcountry Trails

Rocky Mountain National Park: Kawuneeche Valley (E); Shipler Park (E); East Inlet (E); Big Meadows (E); Baker Gulch (M).

The west side Park Administration office is located north of Grand Lake at 16018 U.S. 34, Grand Lake, 80447, 627-3471.

Granby area: Arapaho Creek (EMD).

Fraser Experimental Forest: Deadhorse Creek* (M); West St. Louis Creek* (MD); Morse Mountain (MD); Crooked Creek (MD).

Winter Park area: Jim Creek (EMD); Second Creek (MD); Sevenmile Ski Trail (D).

The Sulphur Ranger District—Arapaho NF, Hwys 40 and 34, Granby, 80446, 887-3331—admisters the above.

Gore Pass area: Gore Creek (EM); French Creek (MD).

Williams Fork area: Kinney Creek** (M); Ute Pass** (MD); Denver Water Board ** (EM); Simpson Creek** (M).

The Middle Park Ranger District—Arapaho NF, 210 S 6th, Kremmling, 80459, 724-3244—administers the above.

* Shown on Eagle Eye's NEDERLAND-GEORGETOWN map.
** Shown on Eagle Eye's FRISCO-BRECKENRIDGE map.

(E) Easier, (M) Moderate, (D) Difficult.

Front Range

The Front Range's cross-country operations include Colorado Outward Bound and the Outdoor Training Leadership Seminars headquartered in Denver, the Boulder Outdoor Center and the Colorado Grand Tour operating from Boulder, Eldora Ski Touring Center outside Nederland, the Gilpin County Outfitters in Central City, the Lazy H and Peaceful Valley ranches near Allenspark, Rocky Mountain Ski Tours operating from Estes Park, and Beaver Meadows located northwest of Fort Collins.

These centers are situated at a relatively high elevation and close to the Continental Divide, near the Roosevelt National Forest. Windblown snow accumulates on the leeward side of the Divide, providing the area with more than adequate snow for good skiing. The various guides and outdoor programs take advantage of the close proximity and the easy access to these backcountry locations.

In the late 1800s, a variety of mining operations sprung up throughout the Front Range. Towns such as Central City, Idaho Springs, and Georgetown were built by eastern investors, lured by the promise of riches from silver and gold. As the mining industry waned in the early to mid-1900s, many towns switched to tourism for their livelihood. The large population of the Denver metro area can now escape to quiet mountain hideaways, especially during the week.

When snowfall is abundant, Golden Gate State Park, west of Golden, provides trails for cross-country skiing.

From Denver, Boulder is reached by U.S. 36, which continues to Estes Park. Nederland and Eldora are 20 miles west of Boulder through Boulder Canyon on Colorado 119. Colorado 72 can be picked up in Nederland and leads to Allenspark to the north and Central City, via Colorado 119, to the south. Central City can also be reached from Interstate 70 by taking Exit 244 to U.S. 6 east, and picking up Colorado 119. Fort Collins is directly north of Denver on Interstate 25. Major airlines, Amtrak and Continental Trailways buses serve Denver. RTD, the Denver metro mass transit bus line, serves some of the outlying areas.

See Map on Page 20

Beaver Meadows

Beaver Meadows is located at what was originally a dude ranch. The present resort complex began with the remaking of the Alpine Country Inn (formerly the Painted Post Ranch House) into a restaurant and lounge. The cross-country ski program was first begun in 1979.

Beaver Meadows is a family-oriented resort and caters to groups from churches, colleges and special retreats. Since the resort is fairly isolated, not much nightlife is available.

Ice skating, snow tubing and sauna facilities are also provided at Beaver Meadows. Rentals for these activities can be found at the ski shop. The skating rink is lighted and has a fire pit for bonfires on cold nights. Beaver Meadows has been the site for some community-sponsored cross-country ski races in the past.

Beaver Meadows is located on the North Fork of the Cache La Poudre River in the Roosevelt National Forest. The elevation is 8,300 ft.

TRAILS

The trails at Beaver Meadows are rated moderate in comparison to those of other touring centers mentioned in this book.

Twenty-five kilometers of groomed and tracked trails are maintained, and all are well-marked with location maps at intersections. The trails begin on ranch property but cover mainly National Forest land. The majority of them cross intermediate terrain; there are also a long beginner's trail

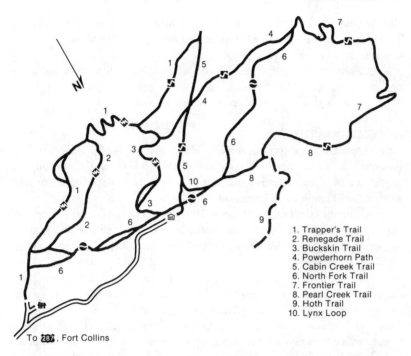

1. Trapper's Trail
2. Renegade Trail
3. Buckskin Trail
4. Powderhorn Path
5. Cabin Creek Trail
6. North Fork Trail
7. Frontier Trail
8. Pearl Creek Trail
9. Hoth Trail
10. Lynx Loop

To 287, Fort Collins

and some short advanced runs. There is no access from these trails to back-country trails.

A warming hut along the trails, staffed on weekends, sells quick hot snacks, such as hot dogs and chili. Restrooms are provided.

Trails are open from 9 a.m. to 4 p.m. seven days a week. Prices for use of the trails are $5 for a one-day ski pass, $12 for three consecutive days, and $20 for seven consecutive days. The fee for children and senior citizens is $2.50 per day. Season trail passes are available for $65 for family members and $35 for individuals.

RENTALS AND INSTRUCTION

Beaver Meadows has a ski shop equipped with 100 pairs of Trak skis. These skis are mostly waxless touring skis, though a few waxable skis are available. The ski shop also carries basic skiing necessities, snack foods, and ice-skating and tubing rentals.

Ski rentals for a half day cost $5; for a full day, $7; and for two days, $12.

Lessons are taught by Fred Leissler, a PSIA-certified instructor and the ski school director. There are two other instructors available to teach classes for all abilities during the season. On Saturdays, Sundays and holidays, two-hour lessons are given at 10 a.m. and at 1:30 p.m. Instruction is offered all other days by appointment. A small amount of telemarking terrain can be found at Beaver Meadows. Group lessons cost $6 per session; private lessons are $12 per lesson.

Moonlight guided tours can be arranged for $5 per person. A ski package, including a half-hour lesson, ski rental, a trail pass and lunch, costs $12.50 weekdays or $16 on weekends and holidays.

ACCOMMODATIONS

Condominiums and cabins are available for rent at Beaver Meadows. The condominiums have one or two bedrooms and two baths. Cabins come in studio and two-bedroom sizes. All rentals have fully equipped kitchens and electric heat; some have fireplaces.

Prices for the condominiums range from $14.50 to $27.50 per person per night, depending on the size of the condominium, the number of people staying, and the season. Cabin prices range from $15 to $25.50 per person per night for the studio cabin and from $14.50 to $27.50 per person per night for the two-bedroom cabins, also depending on occupancy and season. Special rates are available for groups of 10 or more. Meeting and banquet rooms can be reserved for groups as large as 70 people.

Beaver Meadows has a special rate for mid-week skiers, called the Ski Sneak, which includes a three-day ski pass, rentals, ice skating, dinner at the Alpine Inn, and two nights in one of the condominiums for $60 per person. Other package prices are available.

The Alpine Country Inn, open year round for breakfast, lunch and dinner, serves ranch-style meals. The inn, located adjacent to the cabins and condominiums, also features a full-service cocktail lounge.

ACCESS

From Fort Collins, take Colorado 14 north to U.S. 287 and follow U.S. 287 until you reach the Forks Cafe. Here turn left and go northwest past Red Feather Lakes. Take the right fork and proceed about 5 miles to a sign for Beaver Meadows on the left.

Contact Continental Realty, P.O. Box 2167-EE, Fort Collins, Co. 80522, (303) 482-1845.

Eldora Touring Center

Skiers have been using Eldora Touring Center's trails since the 1960s, when the ski team from the University of Colorado at Boulder set track. The touring center became part of Eldora Ski Area in the late 1970s and since 1982 has been a full-service track center. The touring center's main emphasis is on high-quality tracking; racers train on these trails as they are so well-maintained.

Andy Cookler, trail manager with Eldora since 1983, has been working to improve the quality of the trails and to add to the variety of skiing available. He is especially happy to be able to offer backcountry skiing in a "protected wilderness" setting (patrolled daily).

Eldora Touring Center is a member of the Colorado Cross Country Ski Association.

TRAILS

The trails at Eldora Touring Center are moderate in comparison to those of other touring centers mentioned in this book.

The trailhead is at 9,400 ft. There are nearly 40 km of trails, 15 km of which are maintained. Although snowfall can be scarce at Eldora, the trails have been manicured so they can be maintained and skied at any time. The maintained trails are groomed often, sometimes every day. A full range of skiing is available: the majority of trails are intermediate and advanced, and the lower groomed trails provide good beginner skiing.

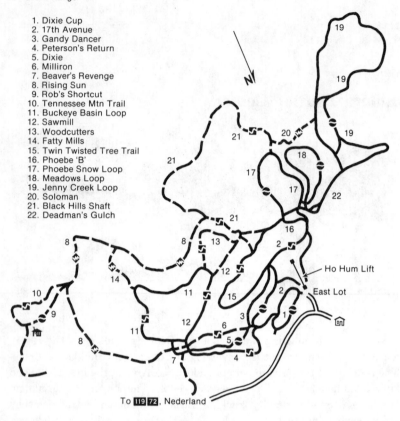

1. Dixie Cup
2. 17th Avenue
3. Gandy Dancer
4. Peterson's Return
5. Dixie
6. Milliron
7. Beaver's Revenge
8. Rising Sun
9. Rob's Shortcut
10. Tennessee Mtn Trail
11. Buckeye Basin Loop
12. Sawmill
13. Woodcutters
14. Fatty Mills
15. Twin Twisted Tree Trail
16. Phoebe 'B'
17. Phoebe Snow Loop
18. Meadows Loop
19. Jenny Creek Loop
20. Soloman
21. Black Hills Shaft
22. Deadman's Gulch

Ho Hum Lift

East Lot

To 119 72, Nederland

The remaining trails, close to 25 km, are not groomed and are allowed to remain in a more natural state. These trails are well marked by blue diamonds. The natural trails allow you to experience skiing in the backcountry in a "protected wilderness" situation. It is a protected situation in that the ski patrol checks the trails daily, and a system for signing in and out at the ski patrol office keeps them apprised of how many skiers are on the trails at all times. There is no avalanche danger on these trails, although some of them pass through fairly rugged terrain.

Eldora has its own hut, the Tennessee Mountain Cabin, which can be rented for overnight stays. The only motorized tool used in the construction of this hand-built log cabin was a chainsaw. It is heated by a woodstove, and wood is provided. The cost depends upon when the cabin is rented and the amount of skiers using it—the $20-to-$30 price range is for the cabin, not per person. The price includes trail passes.

A trailside cafe provides an area for skiers to warm up and buy prepared meals.

Trails are groomed and open by 9 a.m. and close at 3 p.m. The bulletin board at the trailhead provides up-to-date information about the trails. Trail fees are $4 for adults, $2 for children 12 and under, and free for those 65 and over. A season pass costs $60.

RENTALS AND INSTRUCTION

The rental program has over 200 pairs of skis available, including children's skis. They are mostly Fischer touring skis, and both waxless and waxable skis are available. Some racing skis are also available. A full-day rental plus a trail pass costs $10.

Eldora Touring Center is a PSIA-certified ski school. Fifteen instructors, some of whom are certified, teach all levels of lessons from beginner to racing and telemarking. Telemark classes are held every day, for any ability level, at 10:15 a.m. and 1:15 p.m.

Package prices are the following: a trail pass, lesson (two-hour group lesson) and rentals cost $15, a half-day group lesson and trail pass cost $12.

Eldora Touring Center offers several clinics, including women's clinics, telemark clinics, and racing clinics. The women's clinic, for either nordic, alpine or telemark skiing, includes a free nursery or a supervised preschool ski program. The program covers skiing techniques as well as ways to overcome mental obstacles to good skiing. Three clinics are given one day a week for three weeks and include videos, snacks, presentations and afternoon skiing with the instructor. The cost, including rentals and trail passes, is $61, or $45 without rentals.

The telemark clinics are many and varied. The first Saturday of every month, at 10 a.m., four hours of instruction, including videos, are given. The second Saturday of every month, a telemark racing clinic is held, including a four-hour lesson and videos. There will be a fee for the Saturday telemark clinics starting in 1985-86. The Learn to Turn program is held, for no charge, on Tuesday evenings twice a month (downhill slopes are illuminated at night) and includes group telemark lessons. A telemark weekend in early March offers special prices on lift tickets and an all-day racing clinic for advanced telemarkers, including videos and a video critique. A mogul contest is run on the second day of the clinic and prizes are awarded. The price is $27.

The cross-country workshop helps skiers to increase their proficiency in flat-track skiing. Outdoor and cross-country skills are covered for all levels of ability. Held four times during the winter, the workshop costs $22 per session, including a trail pass.

Eldora also holds a racing clinic which teaches techniques for faster, more efficient skiing—skating, uphill, downhill and cornering techniques, and rhythm and momentum.

Senior citizens in the area can join the three-week ski program, held on consecutive Mondays, to learn how to ski or to improve their technique. The trail pass and lesson costs $8, or $13 with rentals. Transportation is provided by bus from local cities at a low cost.

GUIDED TOURS

Guided tours are available at Eldora Touring Center and the destination is chosen according to the abilities of the skiers in each group. Tours can include trips along the lower maintained trails or up to Tennessee Mountain Cabin.

RACES AND SPECIAL EVENTS

Eldora has a busy race schedule. Every Wednesday from December to March, a low-key 5 km or 10 km time trial race is held. There is a small entry fee and no awards are given. The races provide friendly competition and help to improve racing techniques.

Before Christmas, a 10 km race called the Lake Eldora 10K is held. In January, the USSA sponsors a 16 km and 32 km race. Local media sponsors the Eldora Boulder Valley 10K Race in early February. The Rising Sun Classic, held in early March, tests mountaineering skills, such as boiling water, building a snow cave, getting in and out of a sleeping bag, telemarking, and frying and eating two eggs. Oh yes, you have to ski, too. The Boulder County Classic 10K and Telemark Race in late March includes a relay race, an individual 5 km race, and telemark races for teams and individuals.

FOOD AND LODGING

The ski lodge at Eldora provides a lounge and a cafeteria for quick meals. Restaurants and overnight accommodations are located in nearby Nederland and in Boulder, 35 miles away.

ACCESS

From Boulder take Colorado 119 to Nederland. Follow Colorado 119 south through Nederland, to the Eldora turnoff. Follow signs to Eldora Ski Area; the trailhead is in the east parking lot.

Contact Andy Cookler, Eldora Touring Center, P.O. Box 430-EE, Nederland, Co. 80466, (303) 447-8013.

Gilpin County Outfitters

Gilpin County Outfitters has been owned and operated by Bill and Debbie Ward since 1980. The Outfitters are located on a 350-acre ranch two miles northwest of Central City surrounded by the Arapaho National Forest. This is a working ranch which the Wards caretake year round.

TRAILS AND TOURS

The maintained trails on this ranch are rated easier to moderate in comparison to those of other touring centers mentioned in this book.

Gilpin County Outfitters maintain 20 km of trails on the ranch. Most of the trails are beginner and intermediate trails; there is very little advanced terrain. These trails cross the ranch's meadows and stretch over rolling hills and into the surrounding forests. The amount of snowfall each year varies and the wind can be very strong at times, so grooming trails can be difficult. There is no charge for skiing the trails on days with little snow and high winds; the trail fee is $2 when trails are groomed.

Guided tours are an alternative to trail skiing. Bill Ward is knowledgeable about several backcountry trails in the neighboring mountains and forests, where snow is plentiful. These trails start from the abandoned mining town of Apex, at 9,800 ft., eight miles from the ranch. Trails follow old mining, jeep and logging roads, are not marked, and can reach as high as 13,000 feet.

Ward can also guide groups on hut tours. He has access to three separate huts in the Arapaho National Forest. The tour leaves Apex and travels

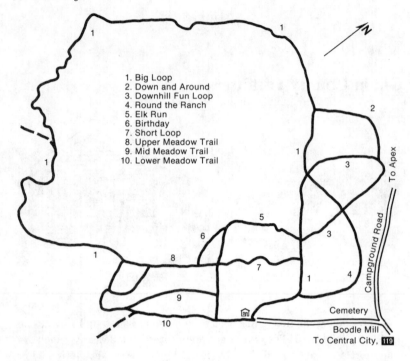

1. Big Loop
2. Down and Around
3. Downhill Fun Loop
4. Round the Ranch
5. Elk Run
6. Birthday
7. Short Loop
8. Upper Meadow Trail
9. Mid Meadow Trail
10. Lower Meadow Trail

two miles up to the first cabin. This is actually a 10-room lodge built in the 1870s with four bedrooms and an indoor bathroom (running water is unavailable in the winter, though water is available outside). The elevation here is 10,600 ft. Skiers can leave directly from this hut or continue three miles farther to the second hut, an old miner's cabin built of rocks, at an elevation of 10,400 ft. The next hut, at 10,000 ft., is four miles away and is another old miner's cabin, built of wood, at a working gold mine.

These tours can include meals or you may provide your own food. Ward can guide six to eight people at one time. Prices for the tour, with meals, per person, are: one night, $45; two nights, $75; three nights, $100; and four nights, $120. Without meals the prices are: one night, $25; two nights, $45; three nights, $60; and four nights, $75. A wide variety of skiing is possible on these tours and groups can choose the type of tour they would like. For example, many groups ski to the first lodge, where they stay overnight, spend time skiing, and then take an alternative route home.

GUIDES AND RENTALS

At this time Ward is the only full-time instructor and guide. He is working on his PSIA certification, is certified in emergency services and avalanche training, and works with the local Search and Rescue squad. He can teach beginning through telemark skiing. Other guides are hired for larger groups.

Gilpin County Outfitters has a full rental program with over 50 pairs of skis available. Trak and Bonna medium touring and mountaineering skis with metal edges can be rented with high touring boots. All skis are waxless. Ward can outfit children two years and older. A full set of ski equipment costs $8.50 per day.

FOOD AND LODGING

After a day of skiing, you may want to enjoy one of the fine restaurants and hotels in Central City, a 19th-century gold mining town. Now a National Historic District, there are still working gold mines around Central City. Almost all of the buildings in the town have been preserved and have kept the flavor of the old west. One hotel, the Golden Rose Hotel, has been restored and decorated in Victorian style. Golden Rose Hotel and Gilpin County Outfitters offer a cross-country ski package.

ACCESS

From Interstate 70 take U.S. 6 west to Golden, then take Colorado 119 north to Black Hawk. Turn off at Black Hawk and follow that road to Central City. Go through the city, and continue two miles to the Boodle Gold Mill and turn left along the chain-link fence. Follow the road between the fence and cemetery for one mile to the blue ranch house at the end of the road.

Contact Bill and Debbie Ward, Gilpin County Outfitters, P.O. Box 64-EE, Central City, Co. 80427, (303) 582-5482.

Lazy H Ranch

Lazy H has been a ranch, though under several other names, since the 1930s when it supplied Lowry Air Force Base, near Denver, with milk before and during World War II. It was also associated with attempts to start an alpine ski area in Allenspark. Old ski trails and an old ski jump can still be seen from the ranch.

In 1978 Lazy H was bought by Bill Halligan, who worked at ski areas and on dude ranches in Montana and Colorado, honing his skills for his own cross-country ski and dude ranch.

Lazy H, at 8,400 ft., is close to Rocky Mountain National Park, where you can ski backcountry trails and drive scenic roads in the winter.

Lazy H is a member of the Colorado Cross Country Ski Association.

TRAILS

The trails at Lazy H are rated easier to moderate in comparison to those of other touring centers mentioned in this book.

Halligan has packed close to 7 km of trails on the ranch in the past. Plans for the future include the acquisition of a tracking machine, and providing set track on several trails. The trails are on mostly beginning and intermediate terrain, crossing open meadows.

Backcountry trails abound in this area, including summer horse trails and National Forest trails such as Brainard Lake, Rock Creek, Bear Lake, and Wild Basin (the last two are in Rocky Mountain National Park). There are many other local trails. Guides are available for tours on these trails,

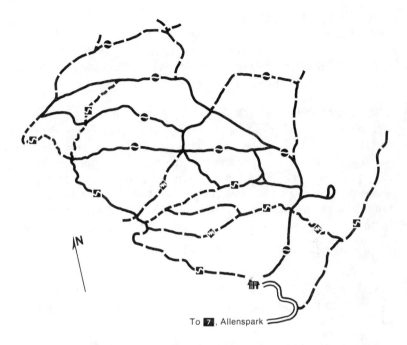

To **7**, Allenspark

if needed, and their services are included in the price of the stay at the ranch.

ACCOMMODATIONS

All guests stay in the main lodge during the winter, where the capacity is 35 people. (Cabins are available in the summer.) Guest rooms are of various sizes; each has been designed differently, some with antiques. All rooms have their own baths. A lovely suite on the third floor over the dining room has huge windows overlooking Rock Creek valley and is adorned with plants. The rooms are classified as economy, regular and deluxe, and prices depend on the length of stay. The price range is from $35 per night for one night in an economy room to $98 for a deluxe room on a two-day package.

The lodge has a hot tub and sauna, a family room, library, and a cocktail lounge called The Saloon. The recreation hall features pool and ping-pong tables, video games, television and a VCR. Snow tubing is also available. The use of all these is included in the nightly rates.

The American, Modified American, and European plans, though none of the rooms have their own kitchen facilities, are all available during the winter. (The Fawn Brook Inn, in Allenspark, serves meals on weekends.) All meals are served in a beautiful pine-paneled dining room, which also overlooks the Rock Creek valley. Meals are served family-style and you are given all you can eat. Meal charges are separate from room prices, though you may plan ahead and pay for all at once. A sample of the meal prices for adults for one day are: American Plan, $20; Modified American Plan, $13.50. Children under two years are served free of charge, and there are two separate categories for other children's prices.

RENTALS AND INSTRUCTION

There are ski rentals available: 15 pairs of waxless touring skis and 18 pairs of medium heavy boots can be rented. If they do not have your size, Lazy H can make arrangements for you with other rental outlets. The cost for rentals is $8 per day, and is not included in the lodging price.

There are two instructors, both of whom worked at Eldora Ski Area and have over 10 years of skiing experience each. All levels of skiing, from beginning to telemarking, are taught. Instruction is included in the lodging price.

ACCESS

From Boulder, take U.S. 36 to Lyons, and turn left onto Colorado 7 in Lyons. Travel 18 miles on Colorado 7 to the ranch, just before Allenspark.

Contact Bill Halligan, Lazy H Ranch, P.O. Box 248-E, Allenspark, Co. 80510, (303) 747-2532.

Peaceful Valley Ski Ranch

Peaceful Valley Ski Ranch, at 8,474 ft., is owned and run by Karl and Mabel Boehm and family. Boehm, from Austria, was a member of the Tenth Mountain Division in World War II. In 1952 he bought Peaceful Valley, which was a stagecoach stop in the 1800s, and designed the ranch to reflect the styles of his home country. Boehm built the main lodge by himself, with pine-paneling in many of the large and private rooms and the outdoor scrollwork found on Austrian alpine homes. Mabel, from Beria, Kentucky, has been in charge of the kitchen since the ranch's beginning.

This is a large ranch, with an enormous lodge and many cabins and buildings for guest accommodations, ranch activities and entertainment. Perched on a hill overlooking the ranch is a chapel where weddings and Sunday services are held. The ranch has an indoor, solar-heated swimming pool, a sauna and whirlpool, a game room with ping-pong and pool tables, a ski shop, and a dancehall. Meeting and conference facilities are available. Those interested in alpine skiing can do so at Eldora Ski Area, 20 miles away in Nederland.

Though there is no organized childcare at the ranch, babysitting services can be arranged.

Peaceful Valley Ski Ranch is a member of the Colorado Cross Country Ski Association.

TRAILS

The skiing at Peaceful Valley Ski Ranch is moderate in comparison to that of other touring centers mentioned in this book.

Though there are no maintained trails on the ranch, backcountry trails in Roosevelt National Forest adjoin ranch property. The trails most frequently used are Beaver Reservoir, Brainard Lakes Trail, Middle St. Vrain Trail, and Bunce School Road. Although the trails are not maintained, they are used often enough so that breaking trail is infrequent. Forest Service trails are marked where they might be confusing. No fees are charged for use of these trails.

ACCOMMODATIONS

The capacity at Peaceful Valley Ski Ranch is 100 people during the winter. Guests may stay in deluxe or economy rooms in the main lodge or in the Edelweiss Chalet. Rooms are mostly large doubles with private baths, and suites are available for families. The rooms are decorated in the same Austrian-alpine design as the rest of the ranch.

Meals are served in two large pine-paneled dining rooms in the main lodge. These rooms are cozy, heated by woodstoves, and overlook a creek, the neighboring forest and its wildlife. Meals are served family-style and guests are given all they can eat. In winter, only the American Plan is offered. Day skiers can purchase meals if reservations are made.

Peaceful Valley Ski Ranch offers ski packages during the winter. Prices include room, meals, use of all the facilities at the lodge, and either cross-country ski instruction and touring or a lift ticket at and transportation to and from Eldora Ski Area. The three-day package, including all of the above, for economy accommodations is $195 per person; for deluxe accommodations, $217 per person. The five-day economy package is $313.50 per person; deluxe is $358 per person. One-night and seven-night packages are also offered.

RENTALS AND INSTRUCTION

Peaceful Valley Ski Ranch has 50 pairs of waxable touring skis available to rent. Boehm believes in waxing skis and will instruct anyone unfamiliar with it. Ski rentals, not covered in the package price, cost $8 per day.

Boehm is one of the two instructors at Peaceful Valley Ski Ranch; he is certified with PSIA. Lessons are geared toward the beginner or intermediate skier. Before attempting the trails, beginners are taught on a small, flat area of the ranch. Guided tours are given upon request and are led on the same backcountry trails mentioned in the trail section above. Boehm will teach telemark skiing if requested, though there is very little telemarking terrain in the area. There is no charge for instruction or guided tours.

ACCESS

From Denver, take U.S. 36 via Boulder to Lyons. Pick up Colorado 7 west in Lyons and follow that for 15 miles to Colorado 72. Turn left on Colorado 72 and follow for four miles to Peaceful Valley Ski Ranch.

Contact Karl and Mabel Boehm, Peaceful Valley Ski Ranch, Star Route, Lyons, Co. 80540, (303) 747-2582 or (303) 747-2204.

Colorado Outward Bound

Colorado Outward Bound makes it clear to prospective students that the school's courses will challenge them beyond their own preconceived limits, to become the most that they can be. The school believes that what people learn in the wilderness translates to everyday life: "Through Outward Bound, it is possible to obtain a sense of accomplishment and direction necessary to attain important life goals."

Colorado Outward Bound offers cross-country skiing courses and ski-mountaineering courses from its Leadville basecamp, at 10,000 ft. No previous experience is necessary to take these courses. The minimum age is 16, there is no upper age limit, and both men and women are welcome. Programs vary in length to accommodate students' differing schedules.

COURSE DESCRIPTIONS

The Cross Country Skiing Course lasts eight days. Basic skills necessary for lightweight backcountry skiing are covered; flat-track skiing and downhill techniques on cross-country skis are practiced. A few days are spent acquiring winter camping and backcountry first-aid skills. Nights are spent at the basecamp, in snowcaves, or in backcountry huts.

The description in the catalog for the 18-day Mountaineering Course states, "Welcome to our most physically demanding course." Experience is not as much a requirement as are physical and mental preparedness for challenges beyond what most people are used to.

The mountaineering course begins in Leadville, and the first few days are spent acquiring skills on a wide variety of terrain, including forests, alpine bowls and mountain ridges. Shelter construction, cold-weather physiology, avalanche safety and winter ecology are covered. When the students are ready to put their knowledge into practice, they will take an expedition lasting several days during which they learn to build snow shelters. This course also includes a two- or three-day solo ski, an opportunity for reflection and relaxation, and a six to 10 mile marathon on skis.

Colorado Outward Bound also offers alpine mountaineering, whitewater rafting and Canyonlands courses. College credit, corporate development, and mental health programs, as well as special adult courses, are also offered.

Tuition for the eight-day cross-country ski course is $675. The 18-day ski mountaineering course costs $975. All instruction, equipment, food and lodging are included in the tuition.

Contact Colorado Outward Bound School, 945 Pennsylvania Street, Dept. EE, Denver, Co. 80203-3198, (303) 837-0880.

Boulder Outdoor Center

The Boulder Outdoor Center is a guiding outfit that takes its clients on tours into the Indian Peaks Wilderness. Several course/tours are offered, including ski mountaineering, winter camping, basic winter mountaineering, intermediate and advanced winter mountaineering, and snowshoe or ski "extravaganzas." These tours can be custom-made to fit the needs, experience and desires of each group. Some destinations are Rollins Pass, Devil's Thumb Pass, and Brainard Lake.

COURSES

The course most suited for cross-country skiers is the ski mountaineering course. It is basically instructional, so beginner skiers can join the group. This course is given for one, two or three days. The first day covers the basics of ski mountaineering, including equipment, waxing methods, cross-country, navigational and mountaineering techniques, and basic avalanche safety. Skiers are taken to an appropriate location in the Indian Peaks Wilderness to encounter a wide variety of skiing terrain on which to practice techniques.

The two-day tour covers what is taught on the first day and includes making ski turns while carrying heavy packs, telemark turns and techniques, falling, self-arrests on skis and how to ascend steep slopes and cross uncertain terrain. The night is spent in a snow cave on the Continental Divide.

On the third day of the course, newly learned skills are used to cross the Continental Divide. Skiers learn the use of climbing skins and ice axes, and how to use a rope to ascend. In-depth avalanche safety is covered.

The one-day ski mountaineering course costs $57 per person for one to three people, or $47 each for four or more people. The two-day course costs $97 each for one to three people, or $83 each for four or more people. The three-day course costs $149 each for groups of one to three people, or $132 each for four or more.

The winter camping program starts with instruction on food and equipment necessary for winter travel. Skiers are taken to the Roosevelt National Forest to choose their camping site. The afternoon is spent constructing a snow cave, consisting of sleeping nooks and cooking areas, and preparing dinner. High-altitude skiing and the return home conclude this program. The fee is $97 per person for one to three people, or $83 each for four or more people.

Other courses offered at Boulder Outdoor Center teach such winter skills as glissading, ice climbing, rope climbing and snowshoeing. Contact the center for more information about these courses.

GUIDES

All guides at the Boulder Outdoor Center have years of skiing and mountaineering experience. All are qualified by the American Avalanche Institute, have map and orienteering skills, have been trained in first aid and have leadership abilities. The guide-to-client ratio is usually kept at 1-to-4.

ACCESS

Boulder Outdoor Center is located at 2510 N. 47th Street, Boulder, Co. 80301. Contact Brian Brodeur, (303) 444-8420.

Outdoor Training Leadership Seminars

Rick Medrick started the Outdoor Leadership Training Seminars in 1973 as a continuation of his involvement with teaching people to ski and enjoy the outdoors. An alpine instructor and former instructor at the Outward Bound School, Medrick became interested in the "Inner Skiing" approach used in teaching alpine skiing, which he incorporated into his own "Centered Skier" philosophy for both alpine and cross-country skiers.

This teaching approach emphasizes the awareness of the skier's internal processes, such as physical tension, breathing, mental state, and the development of center as well as that of the actual physical learning process. The Centered Skier seminars combine traditional teaching techniques of modeling, imitation, demonstration and practice with each individual's own personal feedback. This feedback comes from each skier carefully observing his or her own actions in order to develop an individual style and technique. Different types of stretching are used in combination with the skier's sensitivity to his or her own state of comfort and balance, and to the variation of the slope and terrain. Lessons begin with graduated exercises, coordinating actions with breathing and minimizing tension. The techniques covered range from flat-track and simple turns to advanced telemark and powder skiing.

SEMINARS

The seminars include one- and two-day cross-country workshops. These classes are held at Eldora Ski Area or on backcountry trails throughout Colorado. The destination for the workshop depends on weather and snow conditions and the abilities of the participants. The workshops cost $40 per person for the one-day course and $75 per person for the two-day course. The workshops can be held in conjunction with a weekend at Diamond J Ranch in Meredith for $150 per person, including meals and lodging. Guided ski tours are offered at various sites around the state and can be given for beginning to advanced skiers for $35 per person.

For more advanced skiers, wilderness skiing excursions are led into the Rawah Wilderness area near Cameron Pass, the Mt. Zirkel Wilderness area near Steamboat Springs, and several other areas. These wilderness courses include instruction in ski touring, safety techniques and snow camping, for $210 per person for a five-day trip. Tours are led along the Tenth Mountain Trail for $350 for five days, including food, lodging and transportation from Aspen. The snow- and ice-climbing workshops are two-day lessons that cover rope handling, belaying, use of ice axes and crampons and more, for $90 per person. A ski-mountaineering expedition takes skiers to the summits of 14,000 ft. mountain peaks, and includes instruction in avalanche awareness, advanced skiing techniques, building snow shelters and winter camping. This costs $325 for a seven-day expedition.

Skiers must provide their own skis and equipment for all tours, and food, when it is not included in the price. Transportation is provided in most cases.

Outdoor Leadership Training Seminars also offers an eight-month instructor-training program that teaches technical skills for skiing and climbing, communication skills, trip planning, and the Centered Skier approach and philosophy. The instructors and guides are all taught by this program and are certified skiers who have skied for 20 years. The permanent staff of three to four instructors keeps their guide-to-skier ratio at 1-to-4.

Contact Rick Medrick, Outdoor Leadership Training Seminars, P.O. Box 20281, Denver, Co. 80220, (303) 333-7831.

Rocky Mountain Ski Tours

Rocky Mountain Ski Tours is the only ski school licensed to teach in Rocky Mountain National Park. Bill Evans, the director, is one of the original cross-country enthusiasts in the Colorado Rockies. He has served many terms as an examiner for PSIA. His eight to 10 instructors are certified with PSIA or are working toward their certification; the school has been a PSIA-certified ski school since 1970. Rocky Mountain Ski Tours is a member of the Colorado Cross Country Ski Association.

The trails used in Rocky Mountain National Park are located west of Estes Park. All levels of terrain are available for lessons and tours. Some of the trails that can be toured are the Glacier Gorge trail complex, Fern Lake trail, and trails that originate from the Bear Lake and Glacier Gorge areas, including Storm Pass, Mills Lake, The Loch, Lake Haiyala, Emerald Lake and others.

Operating from the Outdoor World Sporting Goods Store in Estes Park, Rocky Mountain Ski Tours runs classes from 10 a.m. to 3 p.m. Instruction varies from one-day to three-day classes. The three-day course covers everything from beginner lessons through actual touring with the instructor, including equipment, waxing, flat-track and uphill, downhill and trail skills. The instructor-to-student ratio is never more than 1-to-15. All ages are welcome from eight years and over. You must provide your own lunches, waxes, and transportation to the park.

Instruction rates range from $15 for a one-day class to $40 for a three-day session.

Rocky Mountain Ski Tours also offers day tours, private instruction, a two-weekend instructor's course covering teaching techniques and skiing skills, and a Senior Skis program to assist senior citizens to learn at their own pace. Group lessons can be arranged.

Rentals of both cross-country and downhill skis are available through Outdoor World. Cross-country equipment includes Rossignol and Karhu skis, both waxable and waxless. Over 150 pairs of touring, track and mountaineering skis are available. Cross-country rental prices range from $7.50 for one day to $33 for five days. Rentals with classes range from $6 for one day to $29 for five days. A ski repair shop is available for those with their own skis.

Outdoor World is located at 156 E. Elkhorn Ave. in Estes Park. Contact Bill Evans, Rocky Mountain Ski Tours, P.O. Box 2868, Estes Park, Co. 80517, (303) 586-2114 during the winter season, and (303) 586-2671 off-season.

Colorado Grand Tour

The Colorado Grand Tour is a continuous high-altitude ski trail that covers 88 miles from St. Mary's Glacier to the Vail ski resort. Planned and created by Paul Ramer, this route provides a backcountry skiing experience similar to that of the Haute Route (high route) from Chamonix, France, to Saas-Fee, Switzerland. Although there are no huts or shelters along this route, each day of the tour ends at a major highway or ski resort so overnights may be spent in nearby towns.

This trail is still in its beginning stages; the first time the entire route was skied was in May of 1985. Previous attempts to ski the trail were prevented by stormy weather.

The trail is appropriate for intermediate alpine or nordic skiers in good physical condition with adequate high-mountain experience. Ramer hopes that professionally guided tours will be conducted on the trail in the future. He also hopes that the trail will eventually connect with the Tenth Mountain Trail in Vail to offer skiers close to 200 miles of high-country skiing in Colorado from the Front Range to Aspen or Crested Butte.

The first of eight sections of the trail begins at St. Mary's Glacier and vers nine miles to Berthoud Pass. The second section starts at Berthoud Pass and continues 12 miles to the Henderson trailhead at Berthoud Falls. The third portion of the trail continues 12 miles from the Henderson trailhead to Loveland Basin and Valley ski area. The fourth section covers 10 miles from Loveland ski area to Montezuma; the fifth portion starts at Montezuma and continues 16 miles to Breckenridge. The sixth trail section starts at Breckenridge and continues five miles to Copper Mountain. The seventh section covers six miles from Copper Mountain to Vail Pass, and the final section continues 18 miles from Vail Pass to Vail.

For more information about the Colorado Grand Tour, contact Paul Ramer, Alpine Research, Inc., 1930 Central Avenue #F, Boulder, Co. 80301, (303) 444-0660.

Backcountry Trails

Local snow conditions can vary greatly along the Front Range; inquire with the Forest Service before you decide on an area.

Cameron Pass area: Zimmerman Lake (MD); Montgomery Pass (D).
Chambers Lake area: Long Draw (E); Peterson Lake (E); Chambers Lake Campground (E); Laramie River (EM); Blue Lake (M); Green Ridge (MD); Big South (D).

The Redfeather Ranger District—Roosevelt NF, 1600 N. College Ave., Fort Collins, 80524, 484-0036—administers the above.

Estes Park area: North Fork (E); Crosier Mountain (M); Pole Hill (M); Twin Sisters area (M); Lion Gulch (M); Pierson Trail (M).

The Estes-Poudre Ranger District—Roosevelt NF, 148 Remington St., Fort Collins, 80521, 482-3822—administers the above.

Rocky Mountain National Park: Wild Basin (EMD); Upper Beaver Meadows (E); Bear Lake (E); Glacier Basin Campground (E); Endovalley (M); Storm Pass (M); Emerald Lake (M); Hallowell Park (M); The Loch (MD); Fern Lake (D); Black Lake (D).

The east side Park Administration office is located inside the park on U.S. 36; the address is Estes Park, 80517, 586-2371.

Nederland area: Beaver Reservoir* (E); Lefthand Reservoir* (E); CMC South* (E); Rainbow Lakes* (E); Fourth of July* (E); Jenny Lind* (E); Antelope Ridge (M); Jenny Creek* (EMD); Middle St. Vrain* (EM); Waldrop North* (M); Long Lake* (M); Lost Lake* (M); Mammoth Gulch* (M); Rock Creek* (MD); Meadow Mountain* (MD); Mitchell Lake* (MD); Little

Raven* (MD); Sourdough North* (MD); Sourdough South* (MD); King Lake* (MD); Woodland Lake* (D); Guinn Mountain* (D); Devil's Thumb* (D); Rollins Pass (D); James Peak (D).

The Boulder Ranger District—Roosevelt NF, 2995 Baseline Rd., Rm. 16, Boulder, 80303, 444-6001—administers the above. Other trails in the area include those at Golden Gate State Park.

Idaho Springs area: Fall River* (E); Old Highway 103 (E); South Chicago Creek* (E); Echo Lake* (E); Butler Gulch* (M); Waldorf Road* (M); Bard Creek* (M); Idaho Springs Reservoir* (M); Loveland Pass (M); Grizzly Gulch* (D).

The Clear Creek Ranger District—Arapaho NF, 101 Chicago Creek, Idaho Springs, 80452, 567-2901—administers the above.

Grant area: Geneva Creek* (EM); The Sawtooth* (M); Mill Gulch* (M); Duck Creek* (M); Hall Valley* (M); North Beaver Creek* (M); South Beaver Creek (M); Bruno Gulch (M); Hoosier Creek Loop (M); Meridian Trail (MD); Scott Gomer Creek* (MD); Rosalie Trail (MD); Tanglewood Creek (MD); Kirby Gulch (MD); Shelf Lake (MD); Kenosha Pass East (MD); Geneva Mountain* (D); Burning Bear* (D); Handcart Gulch* (D); Gibson Lake* (D).

The South Platte Ranger District—Pike NF, 393 S. Harlan, Suite 107, Lakewood, 80226, 234-5707—administers the above.

Colorado Springs area: Saylor Park (EM); The Crags (EM); Horsethief Park (D).

The Pikes Peak Ranger District—Pike NF, 320 W. Fillmore, Colorado Springs, 80907, 636-1602—administers the above.

* Shown on Eagle Eye's NEDERLAND-GEORGETOWN map.

(E) Easier, (M) Moderate, (D) Difficult.

Long's Peak 14,255'.

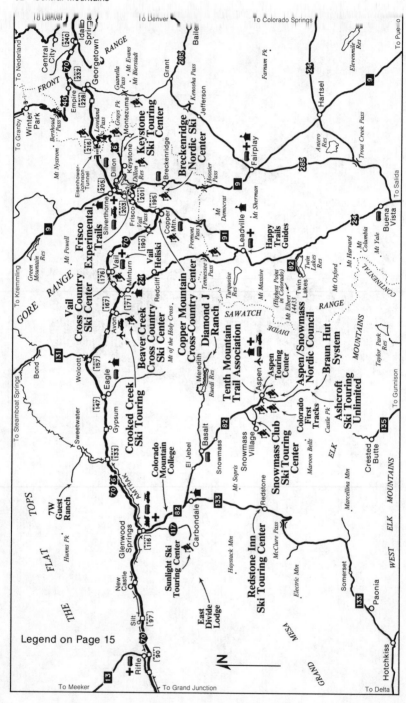

Legend on Page 15

Vail Area — Summit County

The cross-country centers described in this geographic section include the Breckenridge Nordic Center, Copper Mountain Cross-Country Center, Frisco Experimental Trails and Keystone Ski Touring Center located in Summit County, Happy Trails Guides in Leadville, the Vail Cross County Center and Vail Heliski headquartered in Vail, and the Beaver Creek Cross Country Center and Crooked Creek Ski Touring, near Avon.

These centers are close to Interstate 70 and are easily accessible in the winter. Located in the White River and Arapaho national forests, this area is in the midst of the Gore, the Tenmile and the Sawatch mountain ranges and the Holy Cross, Mt. Massive and Eagle's Nest wilderness areas.

The center of Colorado's downhill ski industry, this region boasts six of the busiest ski resorts in the state: Breckenridge, Keystone, Arapahoe Basin, Copper Mountain, Vail and Beaver Creek, plus the first ski area in Colorado—Ski Cooper—on Tennessee Pass near Leadville. Once supported by mining (with silver mines in Leadville and gold mines in Breckenridge), logging (with a logging camp at Copper Mountain) and ranching (throughout the Vail valley), tourism now constitutes its most important industry. The central mountains' livelihood is provided by alpine and nordic skiing, with international alpine competitions; summer hiking, camping and horseback riding; hunting in the fall; and conventions all year round.

Vail's cross-country programs began in the 1960s with the Vail Cross Country Ski Center. Other ski areas soon followed suit by adding nordic programs to their resorts. Frisco, recognizing the importance and growing popularity of the nordic ski industry, is developing its own cross-country resort located just southeast of the town.

Public cross-country skiing trails near Vail can be found at Maloit Park south of Minturn and at the Vail Golf Course. Just outside the town of Leadville are the Silver City trails, the Leadville Fish Hatchery trails, and the Colorado Mountain College Timberline Campus trails.

Breckenridge and Frisco are located at Exit 201 or 203 off Interstate 70; Breckenridge is about 20 miles south of the interstate on Colorado 9. Copper Mountain is at Exit 195; Leadville is reached via Colorado 91 at the same exit. Vail is located 100 miles west of Denver at Exit 176 off the interstate. Rocky Mountain Airways serves the Vail area at a STOLport in Avon. Continental Trailways serves Frisco, Leadville and Vail; the Ski-the-Summit bus connects the Summit County ski resorts, Frisco, Dillon and Silverthorne.

Breckenridge Nordic Ski Center

The Breckenridge Nordic Ski Center consists of maintained trails at two separate areas: the Breckenridge Nordic Ski Center and the Whatley Ranch Cross Country Ski Center. The Nordic Center, at 9,870 ft., is located just one-half mile outside Breckenridge, up Ski Hill Road toward the Peak 8 Ski Area. The trails are on private land and mining claims.

Whatley Ranch, an old homestead located two miles north of Breckenridge, is a private ranch leased to the Nordic Center and connected to it by an 8 km trail. Both centers are run by brothers Gene and Tom Dayton.

The day lodge at the Nordic Center offers rentals, lunches, a warm fire and sundecks and is open daily from 9 a.m. to 4 p.m. The lodge also becomes a center for evening activities, including sleigh rides and Texas-style barbeques, as well as night skiing.

Plans for the future include connecting the trails at the Breckenridge Nordic Ski Center to the Frisco Experimental Trails in Frisco via the Peaks Trail, a U.S. Forest Service backcountry trail.

The Breckenridge Nordic Ski Center is a member of the Colorado Cross Country Ski Association.

TRAILS

The trails at the Breckenridge Nordic Ski Center and the Whatley Ranch Cross Country Ski Center are moderate in comparison to those of other touring centers mentioned in this book.

There are 20 km of maintained trails at the Nordic Center, divided into

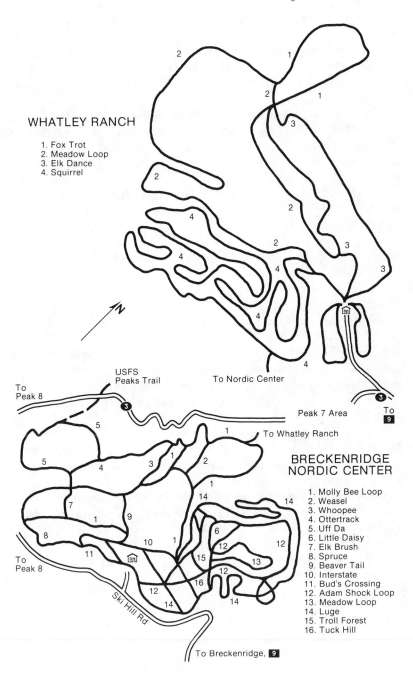

WHATLEY RANCH

1. Fox Trot
2. Meadow Loop
3. Elk Dance
4. Squirrel

USFS
Peaks Trail

To Peak 8

To Nordic Center

Peak 7 Area

To Whatley Ranch

BRECKENRIDGE NORDIC CENTER

1. Molly Bee Loop
2. Weasel
3. Whoopee
4. Ottertrack
5. Uff Da
6. Little Daisy
7. Elk Brush
8. Spruce
9. Beaver Tail
10. Interstate
11. Bud's Crossing
12. Adam Shock Loop
13. Meadow Loop
14. Luge
15. Troll Forest
16. Tuck Hill

To Peak 8

Ski Hill Rd

To Breckenridge, 9

about 40% beginner and 60% intermediate to advanced trails. These are double-tracked, very-well-maintained trails, groomed every day when necessary with state-of-the-art equipment. The trails meander through forests and have several beautiful viewpoints. One trail gives a tour of part of Breckenridge's mining history. The trails are well marked with signs and location maps at trail junctions.

There are 23 km of maintained trails at Whatley Ranch: 2%beginner, 66% intermediate and 32% advanced. These trails stretch across wide-open territory and have their own beautiful vistas. No rental or service facilities are available at Whatley Ranch, though a restored milkhouse can be used as a warming hut.

Trails from the Nordic Center provide access to the Peaks Trail, a Forest Service trail that follows a 10-mile descent along the Tenmile Mountain Range to Frisco.

Trail passes cost $5 for adults and $3 for children 12 and under for a full day. Half-day fares are $4 for adults and $2 for children. Group rates are available.

RENTALS AND INSTRUCTION

Breckenridge Nordic Ski Center has 120 pairs of skis for rent. The majority are Rossignol skis with the Salomon Nordic boot and binding system. Most of the rentals are waxless touring skis, though waxable skis are available. High-performance skis are also available. Skis can be rented at the Breckenridge Nordic Center only. All-day rentals cost $7, half-day rentals are $5, and the weekly package costs $35 including nightly storage. High-performance ski rentals cost $10 a day.

This is a PSIA-certified ski school and some of the six full- and part-time instructors are themselves certified. Lessons include beginner classes through racing classes and provide information on equipment and waxing. Telemark lessons are available at the Breckenridge alpine ski school.

Classes are held every day at 10 a.m. and 2 p.m. Group lessons cost $12; private lessons are available by appointment and are given at 9 a.m. and 1 p.m. The hourly fee for the first person is $25; add $10 for each additional person up to a total of five people. The scheduled lessons are held at the Nordic Center. If lessons are desired at Whatley Ranch, one-day advance notice is required. Prices are the same at both locations.

GUIDED TOURS

The Nordic Ski Party is an evening tour to ghost mines along torch-lit trails at the Nordic Center. Later a fondue party is held in the lodge for a minimum of six people for $16 per person, or $12 each if your own equipment is used.

RACES AND SPECIAL EVENTS

Breckenridge Nordic Ski Center sponsors a 55 km race series each year. The series is divided into three races: the first race, the Father Dyer Gospel Chase in December, is 10 km; the second race, held in January, is the 30 km Klippity Kloppett; and the last, the Nordic Fest, is a 15 km race held in early March. All races take place at the Whatley Ranch. Classes are divided by age and sex and awards are given to winners of each class at the end of each race, as well as to the best overall series winner in each class.

The annual Senior Winter Olympics, an event which has taken place in Summit County for the last three years, was held at the Nordic Center in 1985. Races for the handicapped are also held at the Nordic Center.

FOOD AND LODGING

Numerous restaurants and overnight facilities are located in the town of Breckenridge. For assistance in making reservations, call the Breckenridge Resort Chamber at (800) 221-1091.

Lunches can be purchased at the Nordic Center's day lodge. Lodging and cross-country ski packages are offered by Dayton's Nordic Inn in downtown Breckenridge. The inn has a sauna, dormitory-style rooms and private rooms with shared baths. The shuttle bus stops nearby. Rates include lodging, cross-country equipment, instruction and trail fees. Prices range from $13 to $18 a night for a dorm bed to $29 to $42 a night for a private room, depending on season and occupancy. Groups of 10 or more receive a 10% discount. Call (303) 453-6617.

ACCESS

Take Interstate 70 Exit 201 or 203 and follow Colorado 9 south to Breckenridge. At the Lincoln St. stoplight, take a right-hand turn onto Ski Hill Road and follow a half mile to the Breckenridge Nordic Ski Center on the right. A free shuttle bus provides transportation from Breckenridge and services the touring center.

Contact Gene or Tom Dayton, Breckenridge Nordic Ski Center, P.O. Box 705, Breckenridge, Co. 80424, (303) 453-6855.

Copper Mountain Cross Country Ski Center

The Copper Mountain Cross-Country Center was started in 1972. Operations are conducted from the Union Creek Building at the westernmost end of Copper Mountain Village. Nancy Burke, a young, energetic skier, has directed the touring center since 1982. She originally worked at the resort as a secretary, and passed three stages of the PSIA-certification course in one year to qualify to teach at the center.

Copper Mountain is a member of the Colorado Cross Country Ski Association and has a PSIA-certified ski school.

TRAILS

Trails at Copper Mountain are considered to be more difficult to most difficult in comparison to those of other touring centers mentioned in this book, because of high elevations (9,700 ft. at the base) and a fairly demanding trail system.

Burke maintains 25 km of trails, labeled at junctions and at kilometer marks, which were designed by Dick Taylor, former coach of the U.S. Nordic team and associated with Copper Mountain from 1980-82. Taylor believed in trails with both "stress and rest" stretches, which he incorporated into the trail's design. The majority of trails are intermediate to advanced, though there are nearly 7 km of beginner trails. Well-placed cutoffs allow skiers to make shorter loop trips. All trails are double-tracked, maintained after every snowfall and reset when necessary.

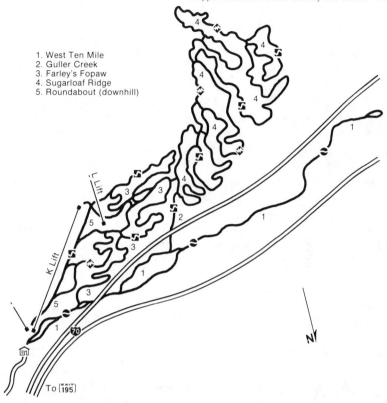

1. West Ten Mile
2. Guller Creek
3. Farley's Fopaw
4. Sugarloaf Ridge
5. Roundabout (downhill)

The K Lift takes you from the base elevation of 9,700 ft. to 10,300 ft. From there you can telemark the downhill trail, Roundabout, or reach Farley's Fopaw and the upper, more advanced trails. Beginner trails are accessible from the Union Creek Building. Access from the trails leads to backcountry skiing at Stafford Creek and Guller Creek.

The touring center is open daily from 8 a.m. to 3:30 p.m.; trails are checked daily at 3:30 p.m. Track fees are $4 for adults and $2 for children, good for one ride on the K Lift. The Combination K Lift/track fee includes unlimited use of the lift and tracks for $7. The Copper Mountain lift ticket is $24 and gives access to the downhill slopes for telemarking.

RENTALS AND INSTRUCTION

Rentals at Copper Mountain include 125 pairs of Trak touring skis, telemarking skis, and children's skis. Touring skis are mostly waxless; telemark skis are waxable. Prices for track skis for a full day are $9 for adults, $6 for children. Track skis for a half day are $7 for adults, $4 for children. Telemark skis for a full day are $12 and $10 for a half day.

There are 12 instructors, 10 of whom are PSIA-certified. All levels of skiing are taught at lessons held from 10:30 a.m. to 12 noon and from 1 p.m. to 2:30 p.m. every day.

The Newcomer Package for $23 includes a group lesson, all-day rentals, and the track fee. Group track lessons for both adults and children for a half day, including track fee, are $15. A one-hour private track or telemark lesson for one person, trail fee included, is $25, plus $10 for an additional person. Telemark lessons for a half day are $15; a lift ticket must be purchased for $5 for first timers. You can trade a day of your Copper Mountain or Ski-the-Summit multiple-day lift ticket for the Newcomer Package at no extra charge.

A Telemark Clinic offers four scheduled days of classes, including beginning, intermediate, advanced and racing telemarking. All aspects of telemarking are covered—position, linked turns, step turns, hop turns, skiing bumps, steep terrain, and powder and racing skills. Videotaping is used in the two more advanced classes. Fees are $20 plus lift ticket for the first two classes; $24 plus lift ticket for the two advanced classes. Telemarking equipment can be rented for $10.

The Women's Series consists of three scheduled days of classes for beginning to intermediate skiers. The series covers track lessons, telemarking and a day-backcountry tour up Mayflower Gulch. This series is subject to change in the future.

The U. S. Ski Coaches Association (USSCA) Track Skiing Clinic is a two-day indoor and outdoor clinic for track skiers. Films and lectures on technique and speed, training, psychology and medical considerations are presented. This clinic qualifies skiers for Level I certification through the USSCA.

The Snow Safety Seminar is a two-day course designed to cover specific snow conditions in the Colorado mountains, including presentations and discussions on mountain meteorology, snow crystal metamorphosis, avalanche dynamics, safe skiing routes, search and rescue, and more. The fee is $40.

GUIDED TOURS

Different types of guided tours can be arranged. Those interested are encouraged to ski with a guide for one day of track skiing and one day of telemark skiing, and then take a day-long backcountry tour. This is suggested for those who have never skied backcountry trails so that guides can assess the abilities of the skiers and then take them on a tour most suitable for their enjoyment. The fee depends on the tour chosen, the length of the tour and the number of skiers.

RACES AND SPECIAL EVENTS

Copper Mountain's major event in mid-January, consists of 7.5 and 20 km races following two of the cross-country trails—Farley's Fopaw and Sugarloaf Ridge. There are feeding stations at the longer 20 km race. Commemorative gifts are given to all participants.

Every Wednesday evening, an introduction to cross-country skiing is presented at the resort from 5:30 to 6:30 p.m. A videotape is shown, followed by discussions about equipment, technique and waxing.

Every Saturday from 9:45 to 10:15 a.m. in the Union Creek Building, a free waxing clinic is offered. Wax of the day, cleaning and waxing skis, and other topics are covered.

FOOD AND LODGING

A cafeteria in the Union Creek Building offers meals and snacks during the day. Copper Mountain Village has a variety of hotel accommodations and restaurants. Copper Mountain Resort Association and Central Reservations, at P.O. Box 3003, Copper Mountain, Co. 80443, (800) 525-3891 (outside Colorado), can assist in making reservations.

Childcare is available; The Belly Button Babies takes infants to two-year-olds, by reservation only. The Belly Button Bakery takes older children, ages two and up. Activities include arts and crafts, baking, science, music and skiing; lunch is provided.

Other activities offered in the village are downhill skiing, sleigh rides, horseback riding, snowmobiling, ice skating, movies, swimming, aerobics, tennis, racketball, and massage.

ACCESS

Copper Mountain is at Exit 195 off Interstate 70. Park in appointed lots and take one of the frequent shuttles to the last west-bound stop on the shuttle line at the Union Creek Building, right at the base of K Lift.

Contact Nancy Burke, Copper Mountain Cross-Country Center, P.O. Box 3001, Copper Mountain, Co. 80443, (303) 968-2882, extension 6301.

Frisco Experimental Trails

Surrounded by alpine ski resorts, Frisco is a town in Summit County with no ski industry of its own. The townspeople recently approved plans to create a cross-country ski resort in Frisco to develop a winter tourist attraction for the small and pretty town. The Bill Koch and Associates' firm was hired, after a design competition, to develop a master plan for this cross-country ski resort. The plan should be completed and approved by January of 1986, with permanent facilities and trails in place by 1986-87.

Because completion of permanent trails and lodge development are not expected until the 1986-87 season, the town initiated the Frisco Experimental Trails Program during the winter of 1985. The program consists of a network of 30 km of regularly groomed and maintained trails. North of Colorado 9, not far from Frisco, track is set in the Peninsula Recreation Area on Dillon Reservoir. South of the highway, set tracks lead directly from town to the Peninsula area with a connection to the Forest Service's Peaks Trail, which continues to Breckenridge. The trails south of the highway are shared with snowmobiles. No fee was charged during the 1985 winter season, however there will be a nominal charge for use of the trails starting in the winter of 1985-86.

The trails are divided into beginner through advanced categories—about 18 km beginner and intermediate and 9 km advanced. Signs mark trail difficulty. Information on the trails, grooming status, and special events is provided at the trailheads. Restroom facilities are available.

Up to 15 km of beginner and intermediate trails to be designed by World Cup champion and Olympic medalist Koch are proposed and pending approval for the 1985-86 season.

The Frisco Gold Rush, a well-attended annual citizens' 10 km race, is held on these trails in February.

Future plans for Frisco include a lodge with rentals and lessons, warming huts along the trails, and retail sales and food services.

ACCESS

Frisco is located on Interstate 70 at Exit 201 or 203. Trails start from the town and at the National Forest Peninsula Campground, two miles east of town on Colorado 9.

Contact Frisco Experimental Trails, P.O. Box 370, Frisco, Co. 80443, or Frisco Town Hall, One Main Street, Frisco, Co. 80443.

Keystone Ski Touring Center

Jana Hlavaty, the touring director at the Keystone Touring Center, was born in Prague, Czechoslovakia, and came to the United States in 1970. After obtaining U.S. citizenship, she competed with the U.S. Olympic nordic team at the 1976 games in Innsbruck, Austria. She joined Keystone Touring Center in 1977 at its beginning when it was located at Keystone Lake. Many of the trails used then are now covered by the expansion of the downhill resort.

The present trails and center were built in 1983. Hlavaty has seen ski touring grow quickly over the past few years; Keystone now includes the new touring center, maintained trails, and plans for improvement and expansion.

Keystone Resort, long advertised as a family resort, attracted beginner skiers; this influenced the development, at Keystone Touring Center, of a ski school oriented toward the novice skier. Although all levels of cross-country skiing are taught at Keystone, the beginner's program is still the most popular.

Keystone Touring Center is a PSIA-certified ski school and a member of the Colorado Cross Country Ski Association.

TRAILS

The trails at Keystone Touring Center are moderate in comparison to those of other touring centers mentioned in this book.

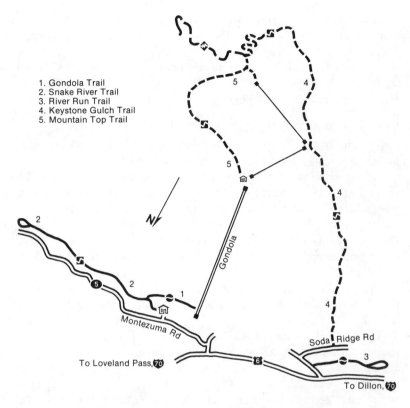

1. Gondola Trail
2. Snake River Trail
3. River Run Trail
4. Keystone Gulch Trail
5. Mountain Top Trail

Thirty-seven kilometers of double-tracked trails are spread over the Keystone area. Two of five trails originate at the touring center, two start at Keystone Village, and the last begins at the River Run Gondola. All the trails are connected by the Keystone shuttle, which also serves Keystone Village and the Keystone Touring Center. Most of the trails are appropriate for beginner and intermediate skiers.

The Mountain Top Trail is reached by taking the River Run Gondola to the Keystone Mountain summit at 11,641 ft. The trail descends around North Peak and into Keystone Gulch. The Tenmile and Gore Mountain ranges are visible from the top of Mountain Top Trail, affording a 360-degree view of Colorado's Rockies. Because it is a full-day trip, skiers are not allowed to begin skiing this trail after noon. The staff has dubbed Mountain Top the "attitude adjustment" trail...a good place to get away from it all. The Summit House, a restaurant at the top of the River Run Gondola, is at present the only place that offers warmth on the Mountain Top Trail. A handout, with safety tips and a description of the trail, is distributed to skiers at the touring center.

If backcountry skiing is desired, drive three to six miles from Keystone Touring Center to Montezuma for a variety of Forest Service trails. The trail fee is $4 and passes are available at the touring center, open daily from 8 a.m. to 5 p.m. One ride up and down the River Run Gondola to the Mountain Top Trail, available to cross-country skiers only, is $8. Telemarkers can ski all of Keystone Mountain for $24.

RENTALS AND INSTRUCTION

Keystone Touring Center has 180 pairs of Salomon waxless touring skis for rent, most with the Salomon Nordic boot and binding system. Waxable skis, telemarking skis and boots, and children's skis are available. The prices for a touring set are $11 for a full day and $8 for a half day. The telemarking set costs $13 for a full day and $10 for a half day.

Fourteen instructors teach at Keystone; the majority are certified by PSIA. Every member of the staff rotates jobs at the touring center, so all are familiar with fitting skis, maintaining trails, and instructing all levels of skiing.

Keystone has an unusually large area for lessons and practice. There are 18 long, straight and flat tracks, as well as a small hill for practicing downhill skills.

Two-hour beginner lessons take place daily at 10 a.m. and 1 p.m.; no reservations are needed. A lesson only is $17; a two-hour lesson including full-day equipment rental and trail fee is $26; a lesson including half-day equipment rental is $21. Downhill skills improvement lessons, at 12:30 to 2 p.m. on Saturday, are $17; lessons including full-day equipment rental are $21. Intermediate lessons, given Saturday from 10:30 a.m. to 12 noon, are $17; lessons including full-day equipment are $21. Private lessons are $30 per hour; a 1-1/2 hour lesson is $38. The cost for additional persons is $7 each. An introduction to telemark turns, given on Tuesdays only from 12:30 to 2 p.m., is $17.

Keystone has a generous policy concerning children's lessons; for example, there is no charge for the child's lesson, when taken with the parent's, if the child has not learned anything. The private-lesson charge for children is $20 for 45 minutes.

The Women's Seminar consists of four consecutive Sundays of track lessons (edging, turning, and balance); improving downhill skills on cross-country skis; refining track and downhill skiing techniques and telemark turn instruction; and a full-day mountain tour with a picnic lunch. The cost is $79 per person and, in addition to lessons, includes trail fees, exercise sessions, hearty lunches and tours.

Telemarking Clinics are offered each Sunday from 10 a.m. to 1 p.m. at Arapahoe Basin. You may register for these clinics at the Keystone Touring Center. The clinic price for a lift ticket, three hours of lessons and a complimentary lunch is $35.

Unstructured racing clinics are given each Thursday on an informal basis. Starting with a group workout, they include different activities, such as timed workouts, each week.

GUIDED TOURS

Half-day tours are scheduled on Mondays and Fridays from 12:30 to 4 p.m. These are easy tours for beginners. The cost is $22 including rentals. Mountain tours are held every Wednesday from 9:30 a.m. to 4 p.m. for $28, or $32 with rentals. Moonlight dinner tours are given (miners' lights are used when the moon is not full), starting with the sunset and rising moon and ending with dinner at Ski Tip Ranch (see below). The $35 price tag includes equipment.

Private tours can be arranged by contacting the Keystone Touring Center 24 hours prior to a desired tour. Most of the tours are conducted from Montezuma on the National Forest trails leading from the town.

RACES AND SPECIAL EVENTS

The Keystone Caper is an annual race held in mid-February since 1974, on the Keystone Golf Course. In 1984, the Caper was the Governor's Cup race when 900 people participated. The 10 km race has 12 classes based on age and sex. Course inspection is allowed the week before the race.

On Mondays, a cross-country ski presentation is given at Keystone Lodge. Movies and equipment are presented and clothing tips and advice on where to ski are discussed.

FOOD AND LODGING

The Ski Tip Ranch, adjacent to the Keystone Touring Center, was built by Max and Edna Dercum on the site of an old stagecoach stop. (Max was a pioneer in American skiing and helped develop both Keystone and Arapahoe Basin.) The lodge contains exposed log walls, two enormous pit fireplaces, low-beamed ceilings and warm and sunny rooms. Keystone Touring Center ends some of their tours at the ranch, and skiers are welcome to enjoy lunch or dinner at the ranch after a day of skiing. Reservations are necessary for dinner. The menu includes homemade soups, breads, and desserts. The dinner entrees change every day and include veal, venison, duck, beef and more. Ask to see the section of the ranch that was once the original building!

Additional restaurants and lodging can be found in Keystone. For help with reservations write Keystone Central Reservations, P.O. Box 38, Keystone, Co. 80435, or call (303) 468-4242 or (303) 534-7712. Activities such as ice skating on Keystone Lake and alpine skiing at Keystone Resort can be enjoyed in town.

ACCESS

On U.S. 6 east of Keystone, look for the sign for Ski Area and Montezuma. (The turnoff is on the Loveland Pass side of Keystone.) Make a turn south at the sign on Montezuma Road (County 5) and follow for about three miles to Keystone Touring Center and Ski Tip Ranch.

Contact Jana Hlavaty, Keystone Touring Center, P.O. Box 38-EE, Keystone, Co. 80435, (303) 468-4275.

Vail/Beaver Creek Cross Country Ski Centers

The first trails open to the public in Vail were at Golden Peak in 1968. Steve Rieschl, who now runs Ambush Ranch, started the touring center and persuaded Jean Naumann, the present director, to become certified to teach and to join the operation. In 1981, Karhu began sponsoring the cross-country center and helped set up a rental program.

More recently, Naumann went to the Lake Tahoe area in California to study touring centers for ideas for the design of the Beaver Creek Cross Country Center. This newest area opened in November of 1984 in McCoy Park above Beaver Creek, and is reached by using one of Beaver Creek's ski lifts.

Both centers are members of the Colorado Cross Country Ski Association and the Cross Country Ski Association of America. The ski schools are certified by PSIA.

TRAILS

Two separate areas offer nordic skiing:

Golden Peak: The trails at Golden Peak are rated easier in comparison to those of other touring centers mentioned in this book.

Golden Peak is located in Vail at the east end of town at the base of Chairlift 6. Lessons are given there and students can practice at the Vail Golf Course or take a guided tour to one of several local backcountry trails. The total distance of set track is 13 km. The Vail Nature Center, operating from the golf course clubhouse, is used as a warming hut. Nordic ski

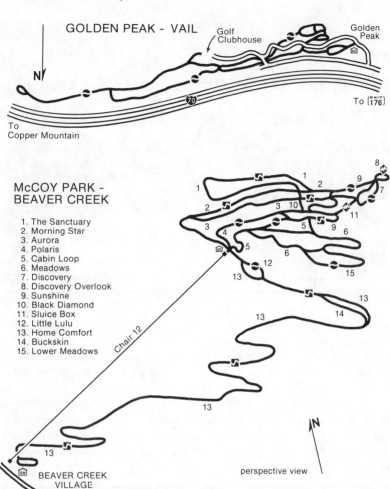

GOLDEN PEAK - VAIL

Golf Clubhouse

Golden Peak

N

To (176)

To Copper Mountain

McCOY PARK - BEAVER CREEK

1. The Sanctuary
2. Morning Star
3. Aurora
4. Polaris
5. Cabin Loop
6. Meadows
7. Discovery
8. Discovery Overlook
9. Sunshine
10. Black Diamond
11. Sluice Box
12. Little Lulu
13. Home Comfort
14. Buckskin
15. Lower Meadows

Chair 12

BEAVER CREEK VILLAGE

To Avon,

perspective view

N

and snowshoe rentals and tours are available. Hours are 9 a.m. to 4 p.m. No dogs are allowed on golf course tracks. There is no trail fee at Vail-Golden Peak.

McCoy Park: The trails at McCoy Park are moderate in comparison to those of other touring centers mentioned in this book.

Cross-country operations at Beaver Creek are conducted from the small building at the base of Lift 12 where rentals and instruction are available. Access to McCoy Park is via Lift 12, a chairlift that takes skiers to 9,840 ft. There, 20 km of 16-ft.-wide double-tracked trails meander through meadows, along ridges and through pine forests. The trails are

30% beginner, 40% intermediate, and 30% advanced; many have been named after mining claims made in the area in the late 1800s. McCoy Park is named for the John F. McCoy homestead, a logging camp before World War I. Spectacular views of the Gore Range and the Gold Dust Peaks can be seen from many parts of these trails. Lake Creek, Bachelor Gulch and Arrowhead, reached from McCoy Park, are places where adventurous skiers can find backcountry skiing. There are no marked trails in these areas.

At present, there is a warming hut at the top of Lift 12 at Beaver Creek. Plans have been made to construct another warming hut at the top of McCoy Park from an old "lettuce barn" that has been preserved. (Lettuce was once grown there for the mining population at Leadville.)

A $10 full-day and $6 half-day access fee is charged for the lift and the trails at Beaver Creek-McCoy Park. A full-day trail fee for children costs $6. The track system at McCoy Park is open from 9 a.m. to 3 p.m.

RENTALS AND INSTRUCTION

Ski equipment can be rented at both Golden Peak and McCoy Park. Seventy pairs of Karhu waxless touring skis, plus 12 pairs of mountaineering skis and six pairs of racing skis, are available at both touring centers. The Contact boot and binding system is used at Beaver Creek, while the three-pin binding system is used at Golden Peak.

Rentals for touring skis are $8, a racing set is $12 and mountaineering skis can be rented for $14. Children's sets cost $8.

Naumann is an examiner for PSIA-Nordic Division and trains the instructors at the Vail/Beaver Creek centers. All the instructors are PSIA-certified or are working on their certification. All levels of skiing instruction are given at both ski centers, from beginning track lessons through advanced telemark clinics. Group or individual lessons can be videotaped upon request.

At Golden Peak, introductory lessons are conducted daily from 10 a.m. to noon. An afternoon tour is held daily from 1:30 to 3:30 p.m., with all-day tours, gourmet tours, and telemark classes held at various times during the week on a regular basis. Check the scheduling at Golden Peak. Private classes can be taken with advance reservation.

Beaver Creek introductory lessons are scheduled every day from 10 a.m. to noon. Afternoon tours are given every day from 1:30 to 3:30 p.m. Telemark tours, all-day tours and private lessons are offered any day with reservations.

A half-day lesson or half-day tour is $17. An all-day class and tour or an all-day tour is $27. Three- and five-day packages cost $72 and $105 respectively. A multiple-day lift ticket at both Vail and Beaver Creek downhill areas may be exchanged for a half-day lesson and equipment rental at either Golden Peak or Beaver Creek. This includes the lift and track fee at McCoy Park. The Vail Valley Card, when bought early in the season is $15; a regular card costs $25. The card allows discounts for various services in town, including $4 off the lift ticket to McCoy Park.

GUIDED TOURS

Surrounding Vail, there are up to 40 backcountry trails used by the guides for tours. These lead from the top of Vail Pass over to Tennessee Pass and down to Squaw Valley. Use of the lifts at Vail provide access to China Bowl and Mushroom Bowl for other tours. The location of each tour is chosen according to the abilities of the skiers, as judged by the guides, and weather conditions.

A gourmet tour is led once a week on Thursdays from the Golden Peak building. This all-day tour, guided by Betsy Robinson, provides a picnic lunch from recipes in her "Red Checkered Picnic Cookbook." An additional lunch fee of $9 is added to the full-day-tour charge for the picnic lunch. Reservations should be made by 4 p.m. the Wednesday before the tour.

RACES AND SPECIAL EVENTS

There are five races a year at Vail/Beaver Creek, starting in early December with Vail Demo Day, which features a demonstration of equipment and free lessons. A Surprise Race at Beaver Creek and the Summit Telemark Series Race at Vail also take place in early December. In March, the Vail Athlete/Beaver Creek 10 km Race and Vail's Pedal, Glide, Stride 5, 5 & 10 km Race (5 km of running, 5 km of cross-country skiing, and 10 km of bicycling) are held. A 20 km race is put on early in April.

FOOD AND LODGING

Vail and Beaver Creek are large resorts that support a huge seasonal influx of skiers each year. Numerous hotels and other housing arrangements can be made for overnight stays. Vail Resort Association-Central Reservations can be reached at 476-5677, in Colorado; 623-6624, toll-free from Denver, and 800-525-3875 outside Colorado. Restaurants are many and varied. After-skiing activities include ice skating in the Dobson Arena in Vail, downhill skiing, heliskiing with Vail Heli-Ski, and Snowcat tours with Resolution SnoTour, (668-5878). The Colorado Ski Museum and the Ski Hall of Fame are open from 12 to 5 p.m. Tuesdays through Sundays; donations are appreciated.

Visitors are asked to park their cars in parking lots provided and use the shuttle buses which serve Beaver Creek through Vail. These buses are warm, prompt and plentiful and the drivers are pleasant and helpful. Buses stop frequently, so walking can be kept to a minimum. Both cross-country centers are stops on the shuttle.

ACCESS

Vail and Beaver Creek are both on Interstate 70. Vail is 100 miles west of Denver at Exit 176, and Avon-Beaver Creek is 10 miles west of Vail at Exit 167. There is a STOLport in Avon into which Rocky Mountain Airways flies frequently.

Contact Jean Naumann, Vail/Beaver Creek Cross Country Ski Centers, 458-G Vail Valley Drive, Vail, Co. 81657, (303) 476-3239, ext. 4380 or (303) 949-5750.

Crooked Creek Ski Touring

Crooked Creek Ski Touring is a cross-country guide service that escorts skiers across the Tenth Mountain Trail from Sylvan Lake (near Eagle) to Aspen. Crooked Creek, south of Crooked Creek Pass, is a group of 12 privately owned cabins built by silver miners, and was originally the center of Crooked Creek Ski Touring. Buck and Holly Elliott started their business there in 1978 as a cross-country resort, to guide groups into the backcountry and instruct all aspects of cross-country skiing. The Elliotts have arrangements with the owners to use the cabins during the winter.

In 1980, Fritz Benedict, an Aspen resident, developed the concept for the Tenth Mountain Trail hut system from Aspen to Vail. Crooked Creek was a logical overnight stop since it was on the trail; it was natural then for Elliott to expand his guide business to escort skiers from Crooked Creek to Aspen. Holly conducts day tours from Vail, which include gourmet lunches using recipes from her cookbook, "The Red Checkered Picnic." Ted Billings, also a guide, has been associated with the Mountaineering School in Vail since 1970 and is Crooked Creek's gourmet chef.

Elliott schedules nine tours during the winter season. Eight people are taken along on each tour. Tours are led by one guide and an assistant, maintaining a comfortable ratio of guides to skiers so the group can split up if necessary. Elliott stresses the quality of the tour...he goes out of his way to help each person enjoy the tour at his or her own pace. The guides carry all food and necessities so skiers can travel under the lighter load of their own personal belongings. Elliott says, "We're here so people can have a better cross-country experience and come to know the finer aspects of a backcountry environment."

Crooked Creek is a member of the Colorado Cross Country Ski Association.

THE TOUR AND HUTS

Crooked Creek plans tours for six days and five nights, beginning on either a Sunday or a Monday. Forty miles are covered. All tour participants are picked up in the Vail area and stop for breakfast in Eagle on the way to the trailhead at Sylvan Lake. After breakfast, the group skis from Sylvan Lake to the Crooked Creek cabin, which, at 9,500 ft., is a seven-mile trip with a 1,500 ft. elevation gain. There is time the first night for sunset touring and telemarking near the cabin.

The next day, the group can practice telemarking as they ski eight miles to the Diamond J Ranch in the Fryingpan Valley at 8,250 ft., a 1,250 ft. elevation loss. At Diamond J there are showers, beds, ranch-style food and a jacuzzi.

The next morning after breakfast, the group skis 10 miles through the Hunter-Fryingpan Wilderness to Margy's Hut at 11,300 ft., a 2,900 ft. elevation gain. (The group's equipment is carried by snowmobile for the first four miles.) The group stays two nights at Margy's and spends the layover day skiing to the summit of Mt. Yeckel (12,000 ft.) for magnificent panoramic views and high-mountain telemarking in Yeckel Bowl. Margy's hut overlooks the Williams Mountains and Spruce Creek, both part of the Hunter-Fryingpan Wilderness.

The group proceeds next to McNamara's Hut, eight miles away at 10,480 ft., first descending 1,700 ft. down Spruce Creek and then climbing 800 ft. up Woody Creek. A sunrise or sunset tour is always planned to Bald Knob for views of the Elk Mountains, the Maroon Bells and Aspen. After being treated to a grand finale gourmet breakfast, the group skis six miles to Aspen, a 2,200 ft. elevation drop. There they are met by the return shuttle and celebrate hut-to-hut skiing with a champagne toast.

The Tenth Mountain huts provide overnight shelter. Sleeping pads, firewood and cooking utensils are stored at the huts. The meals served are special—Elliott and Billings home-dry the food used in their gourmet meals and pride themselves on the homemade breads, soups and stews they create.

Trips include all food, lodging, guides, group equipment, transportation to and from trailheads and a complimentary visor and trip map. The cost for the six-day/five-night tour is $480 per person. Five percent discounts are given to couples and 10% discounts to groups of six or more.

GUIDES

Each tour is headed by a PSIA-certified mountain ski-touring guide. Guides are also qualified in first aid, emergency care and avalanche awareness. Each guide can give complete instruction in trail skiing techniques and telemark turns. Crooked Creek is a PSIA-certified ski school.

PLANNING AHEAD

Crooked Creek helps you plan ahead for this guided tour. Elliott asks each participant to contact him so he can be sure of each skier's competence and physical endurance. He suggests you be at least an intermediate cross-country skier. Skiing the Tenth Mountain Trail is rated more difficult to most difficult in comparison to the skiing at the touring centers mentioned in this book. Elliott wants each person to realize his or her commitment as a participant, to insure a quality skiing experience for and to protect the investment of all the other skiers.

Before you leave home Elliott will send you an organizational packet with an equipment list and recommended manufacturers of equipment, a reservation form, lodging and airline information, and a detailed trip profile (much like the above description). He suggests that you arrive in Vail at least one or two days prior to the departure date to accustom yourself to the altitude and to ski one day with a guide who can assess your skiing abilities. You must carry your own personal belongings, your clothes, and your sleeping bag. Climbing skins are required; you can rent or buy the skins from Crooked Creek Ski Touring.

OTHER TOURS

Private tours on the Tenth Mountain Trail can be arranged and involve from two to six days. Crooked Creek handles all the details. A guide accompanies your group on a two-day and one-night tour for $240. Day guides, for $90 per day, will lead your group to a hut and help pack in supplies.

Crooked Creek offers customized day tours throughout the Vail area for beginning through advanced skiers. Personal instruction in ski touring techniques, including the telemark turn, is provided. Tours are arranged according to skiers' abilities; all tours include a Red Checkered Picnic lunch. The cost is $75 per person for a two-person minimum; $15 for each additional person. Instruction is $30 per hour; $10 per hour for each additional person.

Crooked Creek schedules three weekend tours that emphasize backcountry powder telemark skiing near Crooked Creek Cabin. Information on safe backcountry travel in the winter environment is given. Instruction is provided for both the intermediate and advanced skier. Accommodations are available at Crooked Creek cabin, with meals and sleeping bags and a shuttle for personal equipment. The price is $210 per person with discounts for groups.

For those interested, Crooked Creek will arrange a privately scheduled mountaineering/snow-camping tour for any level of ability. They will arrange all logistics for a trip across Red Table Mountain, a local winter peak ascent, or an extended trek through a remote area of the Colorado Rockies. Inquire for more information.

Contact Buck Elliott, Crooked Creek Ski Touring, P.O. Box 3142-E, Vail, Co. 81658, (303) 476-4123.

Happy Trails Guides

Happy Trails is a ski outfitter and guide service operating at Happy Trails Sporting Goods Store in Leadville. Two guides and instructors escort skiers to several backcountry areas in the Leadville vicinity, including but not limited to Mosquito Pass, the Mt. Zion area, Buckeye Pass, and Ski Cooper. Overnight tours are led to a cabin at the base of Mosquito Pass. The guides have worked at downhill ski areas and are trained in avalanche awareness, advanced first aid and CPR. Skiers of all abilities can be accommodated and tours are arranged according to the skills and desires of those in each group. Tours and lessons are given on a reservation-only basis. Prices depend on the length of the tour, the ability of the skiers and the destination chosen.

Run by Nuell Carrothers, Happy Trails is well equipped to outfit skiers of all types. The equipment provided is kept up-to-date every year. Carrothers carries a full line of Karhu and Kazama skis for rent, including waxless and waxable touring skis, telemarking equipment, racing and demonstration skis, and a full line of equipment for children. He also rents climbing skins, avalanche beacons and other backcountry necessities. Touring skis rent for $7.50 per day, telemark skis are $12.50 per day, racing skis are $10 per day and children's rentals are $5 per day.

Contact Nuell Carrothers, Happy Trails, P.O. Box 818, 508 Harrison Ave., Leadville, Co. 80461, (303) 486-3255.

Vail Heliski

Vail Heliski operates under a United States Forest Service special-use permit for the White River and Arapaho National Forests. Clients are flown to the outer bowls of Vail: Syberia, Two Elk and Super Vail; the Camp Hale area: Sugar Loaf Peak and Chicago Ridge; the Copper Mountain area: Jacque Peak and Tucker Ridge; or the Breckenridge area: Peaks Five and Six and Montezuma Basin.

Skiing with Vail Heliski is for advanced and expert skiers. You are briefed on helicopter skiing procedures, winter and skiing safety, and avalanche warning systems. The guides are qualified by the state of Colorado as mountain guides, and have over 5,000 hours of mountain flying and touring experience.

Tours leave from Vail Pass, Copper Mountain or Montezuma Basin around 9 a.m. and return about 3 p.m. Vail Heliski offers both nordic and alpine ski tours. The nordic tours cost $50 for one helicopter ride to one of the peaks and an all-day guided tour down to town. For alpine skiing, $250 per day buys five ski runs; extra runs are available for $30 each. Groups rates are available.

Contact Whitney Guild, Vail Heliski, P.O. Box 54, Vail, Co. 81658, (303) 949-5113.

Backcountry Trails

Keystone area: Deer Creek* (E); Hunkidori* (M); Webster Pass* (M); Saints John* (M); Peru Creek* (M).
Breckenridge area: French Gulch* (E); Sally Barber Mine* (E); Burro Trail

(E); Bemrose* (EM); McCullough Gulch* (M); Spruce Creek* (M); Boreas Pass* (M); Gold Hill* (M); Pennsylvania Creek (M); Mt. Baldy* (D).

Frisco area: Rainbow Lake* (E); Lily Pad Lake* (E); Corral Creek* (EM); Shrine Pass* (M); Wilder Gulch* (M); Vail Pass East* (M); Mayflower Gulch* (M); Peaks Trail* (M); North Tenmile* (M); Mesa Cortina* (M); South Willow Creek (M); Meadow Creek* (D); Wheeler Lakes* (D).

The Dillon Ranger District—White River NF, 135 Colorado 9, Silverthorne, 80498, 468-5400—administers the above.

Fairplay area: Beaver Creek* (E); Short Loop* (EM); Mineral Park* (EM); Michigan Creek* (EMD); Tie Hack* (MD); Gold Dust* (MD).

The South Park Ranger District—Pike NF, Colorado 9 and U.S. 285, Fairplay, 80440, 836-2404—administers the above.

* Shown on Eagle Eye's FRISCO-BRECKENRIDGE map.

Minturn area: Lower Gilman Road (E); Corral Creek** (EM); Pando Loop** (EM); Camp Hale** (EM); Shrine Pass-Redcliff** (M); No Name Road** (M); Homestake Creek** (M); Tigiwon Trail** (M); Lost Lake** (MD); Spraddle Creek** (MD); Meadow Mountain** (MD); Wearyman Creek (D); Commando Run (D).

The Holy Cross Ranger District—White River NF, 401 Main, Minturn, 81645, 827-5715—administers the above. Other public trails in the area include the Vail Golf Course** (E) and CMC Maloit Park** (E).

Eagle area: Hat Creek** (E); Sylvan Lake** (E); Yeoman Park** (EMD); Fulford Road** (M); Crooked Creek Pass** (MD).

The Eagle Ranger District—White River NF, 125 W. 5th St., Eagle, 81631, 328-6388—administers the above.

Leadville area: Tennessee Pass area (EMD) includes Railroad Run** (E); Lily Lake** (E); Mitchell Creek Loop** (M); Powderhound and Treeline Loops** (M); Long's Gulch** (M); East Tennessee Creek** (M); Slide Lake** (MD) ; Cooper Loop** (D); and Trail of the Tenth (D); Turquoise Lake** (EMD); Clear Creek** (M); Halfmoon Ski Trail** (M); Halfmoon Creek Road** (MD).

The Leadville Ranger District—San Isabel NF, 130 W. 5th St., Leadville, 80461, 486-0749—administers the above. Other public trails in the area include Fish Hatchery** (EMD); CMC Trails** (E); Silver City** (M).

** Shown on Eagle Eye's VAIL-LEADVILLE map.

(E) Easier, (M) Moderate, (D) Difficult.

Aspen Area

Covered in this section are Ashcroft Ski Touring Unlimited, the Aspen/Snowmass Nordic Council, the Braun Hut System, the Tenth Mountain Trail Association, the Aspen Touring Center, and Colorado First Tracks, all located in and around Aspen; the Snowmass Club Ski Touring Center, near Snowmass Village; Colorado Mountain College, East Divide Lodge and Sunlight Ski Touring Center, outside Glenwood Springs; the Redstone Inn Ski Touring Center located in Redstone; the Diamond J Ranch outside the hamlet of Meredith; and the 7W Guest Ranch west of Gypsum near Sweetwater.

Surrounded by the Elk Mountains and the Flat Tops within the White River National Forest, these cross-country centers are located in the Roaring Fork and the Colorado River valleys. Aspen is adjacent to the Maroon Bells-Snowmass Wilderness Area—the Maroon Bells is one of the most beautiful and the most photographed mountains in the United States.

The Aspen area was originally supported by mining interests: coal mining and coking operations near Redstone, marble quarries in Marble outside Redstone, and silver mines in Aspen. Ranching and the tourist trade now help support the towns in the Roaring Fork Valley. Visitors are attracted by the abundant trout fishing, the spectacular hiking trails and campgrounds and the world's largest outdoor natural hot springs pool in Glenwood Springs, established in 1893. President Theodore Roosevelt was one of the many visitors to the Hotel Colorado (also built in 1893, in Glenwood Springs) and hunted with John C. Osgood in Redstone.

Aspen, a silver mining town in the 1880s, has three downhill skiing resorts which had their beginnings in the late 1940s and early 1950s along with the Aspen International Conference Center. Snowmass Ski Resort was opened in 1968. Although the cross-country centers in Aspen and Snowmass are not directly associated with the downhill resorts, the young industry is well supported by the two towns and their residents, proven by the existence of the Aspen/Snowmass Nordic Council, an organization that oversees the maintenance of more than 70 km of cross-country trails in and connecting the two towns.

Aspen is reached by taking Interstate 70 to Exit 116 and following Colorado 82 southeast for 42 miles. Aspen Airways and Rocky Mountain Airways connect Aspen Airport to Denver's Stapleton Airport with several daily flights. Continental Trailways bus serves Glenwood Springs and Aspen. The Pitkin County bus system serves the Roaring Fork Valley from El Jebel to Aspen.

See Map on Page 92

Ashcroft Ski Touring Unlimited

Ashcroft was originally a mining settlement in the 1880s. Once mining and railroads were developed in nearby Aspen, the mining community in Ashcroft faltered and disappeared and Ashcroft became grazing land for cattle. The area has been left relatively untouched since then and the restored historic townsite stands as a monument to the past.

The cross-country ski area was begun in 1971 by Ted Ryan, owner of much of the land in the Ashcroft area. It is now run by Greg Mace, whose father, Stuart Mace, ran dog sleds up the valley years ago.

TRAILS

The trails at Ashcroft Ski Touring Unlimited are rated moderate to more difficult in comparison to those of other touring centers mentioned in this book.

Ashcroft is in a large glacial valley with rolling terrain and spacious open meadows. Mace maintains 30-40 km of trails, utilizing the entire valley— over 700 acres. Many of the trails are double-tracked, but where appropriate they are packed only. There are a fair amount of gentle beginner trails as well as intermediate and advanced ones.

All trails begin at the King Cabin, at 9,500 ft. A ski shop, where trail passes can be purchased and ski equipment rented, is located there. Mace asks that skiers return passes to King Cabin when finished touring, so the staff knows who remains on the trails at all times. He also asks that skiers

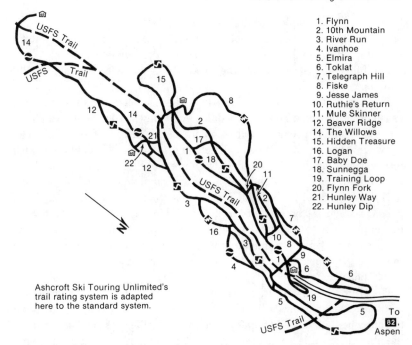

1. Flynn
2. 10th Mountain
3. River Run
4. Ivanhoe
5. Elmira
6. Toklat
7. Telegraph Hill
8. Fiske
9. Jesse James
10. Ruthie's Return
11. Mule Skinner
12. Beaver Ridge
14. The Willows
15. Hidden Treasure
16. Logan
17. Baby Doe
18. Sunnegga
19. Training Loop
20. Flynn Fork
21. Hunley Way
22. Hunley Dip

Ashcroft Ski Touring Unlimited's trail rating system is adapted here to the standard system.

stay on the trails; snow can be very deep and can be the cause of broken equipment and injuries. No dogs are allowed on the trails.

Three warming huts along the trails are furnished with wood-burning stoves, wood, and hot drinks. The Tam O'Shanter Hut, at 9,725 ft., the Hunley Hut and the Kellogg Cabin, at 9,825 ft., are shown on the trail map distributed at King Cabin for your use. Restrooms are located near the Tam O'Shanter, Hunley and Kellogg cabins.

Two avalanche paths cross one of the upper trails. Occasionally, trails are closed because of high avalanche danger; please do not use the trails when they are closed. Since the slopes are ungroomed and snow conditions unpredictable, telemarking cannot be done in this area.

The Braun Hut System trails originate next to Ashcroft Ski Touring Unlimited.

The trail fee for a full day is $7; $4.50 for senior citizens. Children eight and under may ski free. After 1:30 p.m., the half-day fee is $5. Trails are open at 8 a.m. and close at 4 p.m. seven days a week.

RENTALS AND INSTRUCTION

One hundred pairs of Rossignol and Fischer skis, both touring and back-country, can be rented. The staff can give advice on ski waxing and the best skis to rent. A small variety of skiing aids (wax, sun screen, etc.) are sold. There is a complete workshop at King Cabin to help with ski repair and waxing. Skis, boots and poles cost $7.50 for a full day. Backcountry skis are $10 (there are no mountaineering boots available).

One full-time instructor, certified with PSIA and with first-aid qualifications, conducts lessons.

Tours with instruction are offered at King Cabin. The half-day lesson, called the Pine Creek Tour, is scheduled every day at 10 a.m. Starting with basic exercises in prepared tracks, skiers are led into the heart of the valley where they can have a picnic lunch, or to Pine Creek Cookhouse (with reservations required in advance) for a prepared lunch. The lesson lasts 2-1/2 hours; the cost for the trail fee and instruction is $20 per person.

The Kellogg Tour is an all-day intermediate tour, starting at 10 a.m. This lesson is conducted on longer trails and covers instruction in more advanced techniques. The tour pauses at the Kellogg Cabin for lunch. Reservations are needed for this tour and a minimum of four people is required for the tour to begin. The cost for the trail fee, all-day instruction and picnic lunch is $25 per person.

The High Country Tour, an all-day tour for advanced skiers, leaves at 9:30 a.m. The guide leads skiers through the valley into more challenging terrain where advanced techniques are taught. Reservations and a minimum of four people are needed. The cost of the trail fee, the guide and a picnic lunch is $25 per person.

GUIDED TOURS

In addition to the above lesson-tours, several other guided tours are offered. The evening dinner tour leaves the King Cabin at 5:30 p.m., after skiers have been outfitted with skiing equipment and miners' head lamps. You are guided for dinner to the Pine Creek Cookhouse, where a choice of entrees is offered, after which you make the return trip with the aid of your lamp (or the moon). Reservations are needed one day in advance. The price is $30 per person, with a $20 deposit at the time of reservation.

On the Kellogg Overnight Tour, three or four people ski to the Kellogg Cabin using a trail map, after enjoying a picnic lunch. A guide meets the skiers at the cabin, where dinner is cooked and an evening ski tour is a possibility. The next day skiers are on their own again for more skiing. The fee for a picnic lunch, dinner, breakfast, use of the cabin and two days on the trail is $50 per person. Reservations are required.

The Toklat Chalet, for intermediate-or-better skiers, can be reached when weather and snow conditions permit. The Toklat Chalet is a private hut located at timberline toward Pearl Pass. Guides are available but not necessary. Length of stay depends on the skiers. A minimum of six people and reservations are required, with the cost depending on arrangements made.

Other tours include guided trips to Crested Butte, the Goodwin-Greene or Barnard Huts (Braun Huts), or skiing in the Hayden, Star or Cooper bowls. Guides cost $75 for a maximum of five people.

FOOD AND LODGING

Although there is no lodging in Ashcroft, numerous hotels and lodges and a wide variety of restaurants, grocery stores and convenience stores are located nearby in Aspen or Snowmass. The Aspen Resort Association, at (303) 925-9000 or Snowmass Central Reservations at (303) 923-2010 can help with reservations.

The Pine Creek Cookhouse is located a 2.4 km ski from King Cabin. This very small restaurant offers Swiss and Hungarian meals with Austrian, Hungarian, and Italian wines to complement the meal. Lunch and dinner are served, and because of the restaurant's small size, reservations are necessary. The Cookhouse is closed Mondays.

ACCESS

From I-70, take the Glenwood Springs-Aspen Exit 116 and follow Colorado 82 to Maroon Creek Road on the right, just west of Aspen. Take the immediate left turn at the sign pointing to Ashcroft. Follow for 12 miles to the parking area and walk to King Cabin.

High Mountain Taxi in Aspen makes a daily trip to and from Ashcroft. It leaves The Hub, 315 E. Hyman, at 9:15 a.m. and leaves Ashcroft at 4 p.m. The fee is $4 one way; $6 both ways. Ashcroft Ski Touring Unlimited gives a discount on some of their tours upon receipt of a taxi ticket.

Contact Greg Mace, Ashcroft Ski Touring Unlimited, P.O. Box 1572, Aspen, Co. 81612, (303) 925-1971.

Aspen/Snowmass Nordic Council

Aspen/Snowmass Nordic Council is a non-profit organization that coordinates the cross-country skiing in and between the two towns. An amazing 70 km of trails are maintained and can be skied at no charge. Plans for the future have all these trails interconnected so continuous skiing from the east end of Aspen all the way to Snowmass will be possible.

Skiing ranges from easier, at the Aspen Golf Course, to more difficult, at The Snowmass Club, with many kilometers of intermediate trails in between. The entire 70 km are double-tracked and are maintained by the Nordic Council. Several sections of the trails cross private land and skiers' cooperation is asked in staying on the trails, respecting private property and leaving dogs at home. Dogs on leashes are allowed on the Rio Grande Trail only.

TRAILS

The Aspen Club trails are for intermediate skiers and start at Ute Avenue in Aspen and wind through gravel pits to border the North Star nature preserve.

The Rio Grande Trail is an easier tour along the Roaring Fork River from the Aspen Post Office to Slaughterhouse Bridge, continuing to the Airport Business Center on the old railroad corridor.

The Aspen Golf Course trails are mostly flat, easier trails and are located just west of town.

1. Aspen Club Tracks
2. High School Tracks
3. Golf Course Tracks
4. Rio Grande Trail
5. Owl Creek Trail
6. Mountain Edge Trail

The High School Tracks, considered intermediate in difficulty, are at the base of Aspen Highlands and are used by the Aspen Nordic Team for training and racing. The public is welcome to use these trails. The golf course and high school trails are linked, though Highway 82 must be crossed.

The new Mountain Edge Trail is an intermediate trail that links the Aspen Club and the High School Tracks along the base of Aspen Mountain.

The Owl Creek Trail starts at Tiehack, the southeast part of Buttermilk, and runs west across the face of Buttermilk, descending into the Owl Creek drainage. This excellent trail is 8 km long and stretches over meadows and into aspen and pine forests. It eventually meets up with the trail system at the Snowmass Club. An intermediate trail, it is easier to ski from Snowmass to Buttermilk. A new bridge will connect the Owl Creek Trail to the Aspen Golf Course and High School Tracks beginning in the 1985-86 season. Dogs are strictly prohibited as this is an elk migration path.

The Snowmass Club has developed a large system of beginner to advanced trails on the Snowmass Golf Course and above Owl Creek Road.

The Aspen City Council is working on a proposal to set up a ski rental and retail shop, including a ski school, at the Aspen Golf Course clubhouse in the 1985-86 season. The Aspen/Snowmass Nordic Council encourages skiers to use the area's numerous National Forest and public trails as well as the other touring centers and hut systems in the area.

Contact Craig Ward, Executive Director, Aspen/Snowmass Nordic Council, P.O. Box 10815, Aspen, Co. 81612, (303) 925-4790.

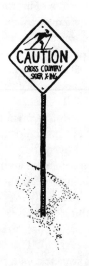

Redstone Inn Ski Touring Center

The Crystal River Valley is one of the prettiest areas in Colorado. As Colorado 133 threads its way from Carbondale to the top of McClure Pass, it travels through farmland, into a narrow and steep river valley and over a pass with a breathtaking view of the Elk Mountains. Redstone is in the center of all this.

The Ute Indians were the original inhabitants of the Crystal River Valley until 1880, when they were driven out entirely by white miners and settlers. Redstone grew around the coal mining and coking operations developed by John C. Osgood in the 1890s. The present Redstone Inn and many of the Redstone houses were built by Osgood for his employees. Cleveholm Manor, now "The Redstone Castle," seen from the highway one mile south of town, was built by Osgood for his wife and is now available for private bookings.

Aside from the inn, two motels and a restaurant serve visitors to Redstone. Food, lodging and alpine skiing are available in Carbondale, Glenwood Springs, and Aspen, all within 50 miles of Redstone. Other activities offered in the vicinity are ice skating on a small pond behind the ski store and dog sledding races at the end of January. A citizens' cross-country ski race, scheduled by the Redstone Inn Ski Touring Center is usually planned sometime in February. Heliskiing is available through Colorado First Tracks in Aspen.

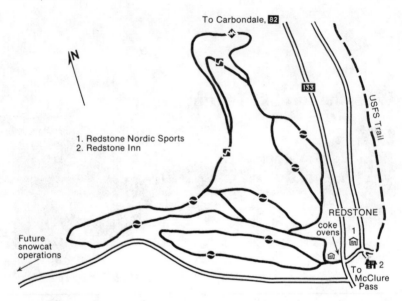

1. Redstone Nordic Sports
2. Redstone Inn

TRAILS

The trails at Redstone Inn Ski Touring Center are moderate in comparison to those of other touring centers mentioned in this book.

The trail system is located across Colorado 133 from the Redstone Inn through a break in the coke ovens that line the highway. There are 15 km of groomed trails, though Bob and Debbie McCormick, who manage the touring center, hope to expand in the future. The trails are mostly beginner and intermediate and are single- and double-tracked. Telemarking is possible only after a fresh snow. Gentle, well-planned trails have been set through pine, aspen and cottonwood trees. There are some steeper spots; from the top of these are views of Chair Mountain and Mt. Sopris. A hut, warmed by a woodstove, is located at the beginning of the trails.

The Redstone Inn is working with the Forest Service to attain a permit to run a snowcat up Spring Creek and Bear Creek Basins, so they can offer telemark and backcountry skiing. As of 1985, surveying and snow studies have taken place. The McCormicks hope to offer guided snowcat skiing by the winter of 1986-87.

Trail fees for adults are $3, children are $1, and season tickets are $25. Guests at the Redstone Inn receive complimentary trail passes.

ACCOMMODATIONS

The Redstone Inn is listed in the National Register of Historic Places. It was renovated in 1983, and because it is a Historic Landmark, 75% of it had to remain original. The Tudor-style inn is decorated by a balcony surrounding the second floor and a four-story clock-tower.

The main floor is a lovely collection of small, cozy rooms—a bar and restaurant, a reading room, a music room and a banquet room—all filled with the original furniture of the inn. For the most part, the second and third floors contain double bedrooms. These have attached baths and are furnished with oak furniture, brass beds, the original light fixtures and such modern conveniences as televisions and telephones. Some of the rooms on the third floor are dormers, most of which share baths. The inn has an outdoor jacuzzi which is open year round.

The inn rates range from $30 for dormers to $72 for a studio with two beds.

No meal plan is offered at the inn. The restaurant serves traditional breakfasts and lunches; the continental dinner menu features entrees of steaks, seafood, veal, lamb and duckling. A champagne buffet brunch is served on Sundays.

RENTALS AND INSTRUCTION

Across the street from the Redstone Inn and down Redstone Boulevard two houses on the left is what was once the "ice house" for Redstone. Now Redstone Nordic Sports, it is the base for cross-country skiing at the Redstone Inn Ski Touring Center. The McCormicks run a ski shop, manage the touring center and sell trail passes there.

There are enough skis for rent to outfit 30 people including children. Skis are mostly Fischer waxless touring skis. Demonstration models are also available to rent. The cost is $9.50 for adults, and $6.50 for children for a full day.

Bob McCormick is the main instructor and is certified with PSIA. He teaches all levels of skiing from beginning to telemarking.

Basic introductory lessons are $5 and are scheduled at 9 a.m. on Saturdays. Private lessons for one to two people cost $20 per hour; a group lesson for a half day costs $15, or $25 for a full day lesson and tour.

GUIDED TOURS

McCormick leads tours, arranged by appointment, up the Crystal River Valley when the weather permits. Avalanche danger can be extremely high in the backcountry. Among the beautiful destinations for guided tours are Marble, the site of an old marble quarry, and McClure Pass. Moonlight tours are a popular request. If visitors wish to ski in the backcountry, several National Forest trails in the vicinity are recommended.

The charge for guided tours is $20 per hour per guide. Small groups are preferred.

ACCESS

Take Interstate I-70 to the Glenwood Springs-Aspen Exit 116 and follow Colorado 82 for 12 miles to the Carbondale, Colorado 133, turnoff. Follow Colorado 133 for 18 miles to signs for Redstone. The Redstone Inn is visible from the highway.

Contact Bob and Debbie McCormick, Redstone Nordic Sports, 0058 Redstone Blvd., Redstone, Co. 81623, (303) 963-3408 or (303) 963-1635.

Snowmass Club Ski Touring Center

The Snowmass Club Touring Center was started at the Snowmass Golf Course in 1970. In 1981 it was purchased by the Snowmass Club and was moved to its present location across from the Snowmass Clubhouse. At the same time, Toby Morse approached the Snowmass Club with a proposal to run the touring center, and has been its director since then. The Snowmass Club, at 8,100 ft., is a private athletic club complete with hotel, restaurant, pools, sauna and tennis courts and is located one mile from Snowmass Village.

The trails are part of the Aspen/Snowmass Nordic Council's network, which consists of 70 km of trails in and between Snowmass and Aspen.

Other winter activities in the Snowmass area are alpine skiing, dog sledding, sleigh rides, and snowshoe tours.

TRAILS

The trails at Snowmass Club Touring Center are rated moderate in comparison to those of other touring centers mentioned in this book.

Trails are open from 8 a.m. to 4:30 p.m. daily, through the December 1 to April 14 season. Morse maintains 38 km of double-tracked trails, which are divided into 8 km of beginner, 20 km of intermediate and 10 km of expert trails. The trails at the Snowmass Golf Course are on land owned by the Snowmass Club and are bordered by the White River National Forest. Plans are now being made to expand the trails up to 40 km by the winter of 1985-86. Morse has hopes that this touring center will grow each year and

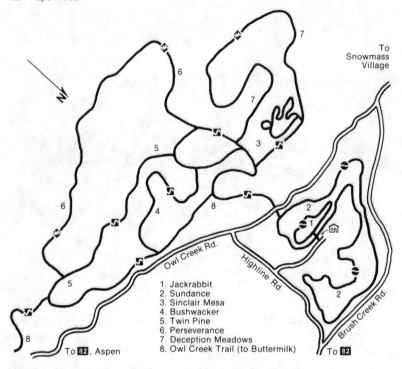

1. Jackrabbit
2. Sundance
3. Sinclair Mesa
4. Bushwacker
5. Twin Pine
6. Perseverance
7. Deception Meadows
8. Owl Creek Trail (to Buttermilk)

become a premier track touring center in Colorado.

All the trails in the Aspen/Snowmass Nordic Council system, including those at the Snowmass Club Touring Center, are free of charge.

RENTALS AND INSTRUCTION

Morse has 80-90 pairs of Rossignol skis for rent, most with Salomon Nordic System boots and bindings. Track skis only are available. A complete rental set costs $8 for a full day, $6 for a half day, $21 for three days, and $32 for five days. Skis rented separately for a full day cost $5; boots, $5; and poles, $2. A small retail shop located at the touring center has cross-country equipment available for purchase; ski tuning costs $8 and includes cleaning and waxing.

This is a PSIA-certified ski school. There are four instructors, one of whom is certified by PSIA. Each instructor has 10 to 12 years of skiing and racing experience and can teach all levels of skiing. Telemarkers are sent to Buttermilk in Aspen, where lessons are available at the Aspen Ski School.

Only one special clinic is held in the beginning of the season at Snowmass Club Touring Center. It covers every aspect of track skiing as a warm-up for the upcoming winter. The clinic is advertised locally.

Beginner group lessons, from 10 a.m. to 12 noon, are $14 per person. Private lessons are given by appointment and all abilities are taught for $20 per hour.

GUIDED TOURS

Snowmass Club Touring Center schedules two types of tours—a full-day tour and a half-day tour. The full-day tour takes place on Thursdays only and lasts from 9 a.m. to 4 p.m. This intermediate 10 km tour begins at the touring center, follows the Owl Creek Trail, and ends at the Buttermilk-Tiehack ski area. The tour costs $40 per person and includes a guide, lunch, and equipment. A minimum of four people is needed for the tour.

The half-day tour is a 7-1/2 km tour which starts at the Touring Center and heads through the upper trails of the East Fork of Brush Creek and into Owl Creek Valley. This tour lasts from 10 a.m. until 2 p.m. and is given daily. A minimum of four persons is needed at a cost of $25 per person. The price includes a guide, lunch and equipment. Gracie's Cabin, a warming hut, is used during these tours but is not open to the general public.

Tours on the Government Trail can be arranged. This is a Forest Service trail adjacent to the Snowmass Club Touring Center trails. Dinner tours and specially arranged private tours are available by appointment.

RACES AND SPECIAL EVENTS

Morse already runs several annual cross-country races and hopes to hold more each year. Three of the events, sponsored by the United States Ski Association, are championship races. These are the Rocky Mountain Division Seniors and Master Relay Championships, held in early January; the Rocky Mountain Division Junior Relay Championships in mid-January; and the Snowmass-Ute Series 30 km Championship Race held in March.

Several citizens' races are scheduled each year. The Annual Silverboom Citizens' 10 km Race has been held during December for 14 years as a benefit for the local junior ski team. Other races are the Snowmass-Ute Series 15 km Race, in January; the Annual Winterskol Balloon Cross Country Race, involving a hot-air balloon ride and a cross-country ski race, held in January during the local Winterskol celebration; the Polk Poke 5 km Race, in February; and the Annual Skinny Ski Social, in April.

Snowmass plans to run an annual April skiing clinic with BOLD (Blind Outdoor Leadership Development), starting in 1985.

FOOD AND LODGING

Snowmass Club Touring Center is located one mile from Snowmass Village, where there is an abundance of accommodations and restaurants. The Snowmass Club, across the street, houses a restaurant and hotel rooms as well as an athletic club. Aspen, with its many lodging facilities and restaurants and its reputation for exciting nightlife, is six miles away. A shuttle bus connects Snowmass and Aspen.

For assistance in finding lodging, contact Snowmass Central Reservations, P.O. Box 5566, Snowmass Village, Co. 81615, (303) 923-2010.

ACCESS

From Interstate 70, take the Glenwood Springs-Aspen Exit 116 and follow Colorado 82 toward Aspen. Take a right turn to Snowmass Village on Brush Creek Road and follow 2-1/2 miles to a left turn onto Highline Road. Follow this for about a half mile and take the first right-hand turn onto Snowmass Club Circle. The Snowmass Club Touring Center is on the left-hand side of the road, past the Snowmass Club.

Contact Toby Morse, Snowmass Club Touring Center, 0239 Snowmass Club Circle, Snowmass Village, Co. 81615, (303) 923-3148 or (303) 923-5600 ext. 151.

Diamond J Ranch

The Fryingpan Valley, where the Diamond J Ranch is located, was homesteaded in the mid-1800s. Diamond J itself was begun by a wrangler, Delbert Bowles, in 1910. The Colorado-Midland Railroad, which traveled over Hagerman Pass through the three-mile Carlton Tunnel to Leadville, had a ticket office on the ranch. The railroad serviced a sawmill in nearby Norrie that cut wood for charcoal shipped to the mines in Leadville. Because visitors soon outnumbered the cattle, Bowles started the guest ranch, which has continued until today.

Diamond J , at 8,300 ft., was bought in 1982 by Bill and Martha Sims, who came to Colorado with their six children in search of a new challenge. From Ohio, the Simses were convinced by one of their sons to move to Colorado, after he had been to school at Colorado Mountain College for ranch management. At that time, Diamond J was a guest ranch but had no cross-country skiing program. The same year the Simses moved to Diamond J, the Tenth Mountain Trail was established and the first stream of skiers began arriving. Half of Diamond J's guests ski the Tenth Mountain Trail and half are week-long guests who ski the trails around the ranch.

A member of the Colorado Cross Country Ski Association, Diamond J is located within 40 miles of five of Colorado's alpine ski areas.

TRAILS

The trails at Diamond J are moderate in comparison to those of other touring centers mentioned in this book.

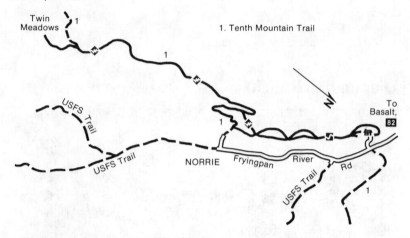

The Simses maintain 19 km of trails around their ranch. The trails are single-tracked, including the portion of the Tenth Mountain Trail to Twin Meadows. All levels of trails are available, though the majority of them are intermediate. Telemarking slopes can be found in the upper meadows surrounding the ranch.

Several Forest Service backcountry trails in the vicinity include Lime Creek Road, the North Fork of the Fryingpan, Hagerman Pass Road, and a trail to Chapman Campground. Miles and miles of skiing terrain are available around Diamond J with little worry of avalanche danger.

Guests ski free of charge. Non-guest track fees are $3; with use of the hot tub or sauna, $5. The non-guest track fee with dinner, hot tub and sauna is $15.

ACCOMMODATIONS

The lodge, built in 1949, was constructed of logs cut from the area surrounding the ranch. It is a warm building with a large lounge area complete with fireplace, and a very long dining room with low ceilings, several dining tables and a built-in china cabinet. The lodge is furnished with old oak furniture. Upstairs are nine bedrooms which share two large bathrooms.

There are several sizes of cabins at Diamond J. 'A' cabins accommodate five or six people and are equipped with a kitchen, a bathroom and a fireplace. Small 'A' cabins accommodate three to four people; these are equipped with a kitchenette, a bathroom and a fireplace. 'B' cabins are rustic cabins with woodstoves only; they accommodate two or three people and guests must use the facilities in the lodge. Hut-type accommodations are also available. These are cabins with cooking facilities, baths, and beds; no linens are provided though showers and towels are furnished. The cabins, scattered around the ranch, are only a short walk from the lodge.

An outdoor jacuzzi and sauna can be used by guests free of charge. The rates for the cabins and rooms are as follows: 'A' cabins, five persons, $450 per week, $90 per day. Small 'A' cabins, three persons, $325 per week, $65 per day. Lodge rooms and 'B' cabins, two persons, $225 per week, $45 per day. An additional adult is $25 per week, $5 per day. Hut accommodations are available for $18 per person per night.

You can either prepare your meals in cabins equipped with kitchens or purchase them at the ranch. The charge for breakfast for an adult is $4.50; 12 and under, $3. Lunch for an adult is $4.50; 12 and under, $3. Dinner for adults is $10; 12 and under, $6.

RENTALS AND INSTRUCTION

There are not many ski rentals at Diamond J, as the demand for them is not great. Most visitors bring their own skis. If the Simses are aware that guests have no equipment and will be spending a week skiing the area, they will suggest a stop at a rental store on the way to the ranch. However, 20 pairs of ski boots and 12 pairs of skis can be rented at the ranch for $3 a set.

Although there are not many requests for skiing instruction, the Simses are qualified to teach all levels of skiing. Jay Zarr, a PSIA-certified ski instructor, teaches or guides skiers on the local trails. Fees for private lessons are $20 per hour for a two-hour minimum. Group lessons are $10 per person for a half-day lesson; four or more people pay $25 each per full day.

GUIDED TOURS

Guided tours are available around Diamond J. The ranch recommends three guide services: Jay Zarr, the local guide, Crooked Creek Ski Touring in Vail, and the Rocky Mountain Climbing School/Aspen Touring Center in Aspen. These are recommended for anyone who is interested in skiing the Tenth Mountain Trail to Aspen. The fees for the Diamond J-to-Aspen tour, guided by Jay Zarr, for a group of one to four people is $125 per day; for a group of eight, $250. Contact Crooked Creek and Aspen Touring Center for their fees.

RACES AND SPECIAL EVENTS

One race is held at Diamond J, the April Fool's Telemarking race, sponsored by the Ute Mountaineer in Aspen.

Snow-tubing, jacuzzi, sauna, a VCR with ski films and a film about the Tenth Mountain Trail are all available at the ranch for guests. Movies can be rented from town.

ACCESS

From Interstate 70, take Glenwood Springs-Aspen Exit 116 and follow Colorado 82 to Basalt. At the light, take a left-hand turn onto the main street in Basalt and follow it as it leaves town. This is Fryingpan Road. Follow this for 26 miles past Ruedi Reservoir and Meredith to Diamond J on the right. Shuttle service is provided by the Simses from Aspen, Snowmass, and Glenwood Springs at $10 per person with a $30 minimum; from Vail, Beaver Creek and Sylvan Lake, $30 per person with a $100 minimium.

Contact Bill and Martha Sims, Diamond J Guest Ranch, 26604 Fryingpan Road, Meredith, Co. 81642, (303) 927-3222.

At Diamond J Ranch.

Colorado Mountain College

The Spring Valley campus of Colorado Mountain College (CMC) at Glenwood Springs offers a program in Outdoor Education and Recreation, which in the winter season includes cross-country skiing. Cross-country skiing is represented in four ways: basic cross-country and telemark classes, from beginning to advanced, are given; PSIA holds clinics and gives exams through CMC; winter mountaineering trips are scheduled; and the American Avalanche Institute offers a four-day professional course once a year through the school. CMC also has its own nordic ski team.

CMC is a regional school with small campuses around Colorado. The main campuses are in Glenwood Springs, Leadville and Steamboat Springs, but college centers are located in a number of other towns where classes are conducted within the college system. Many of these centers hold cross-country ski classes on a demand basis, and the Leadville campus runs a program instructing students to run a cross-country ski center.

The Spring Valley campus offers a full-time and very extensive cross-country program. It is run by Jay Zarr, a forest representative for the Sopris District of the White River National Forest, a trained EMT, an outdoor leader through the Wilderness Education Association, and a local guide for backcountry ski tours. Zarr teaches many of the courses and stresses environmental and ecological awareness in all of them.

COURSE DESCRIPTIONS

The Beginning Nordic Skiing course teaches the basic techniques required for cross-country touring, including route finding and waxing; practice takes place on a variety of terrain.

The Intermediate Nordic Skiing course helps students improve proficiency in track techniques and introduces telemark skiing, racing and backcountry techniques, winter camping skills, advanced waxing, and equipment preparation.

Two courses, called Snow Orientation, are winter mountaineering courses consisting of overnight trips into the backcountry. In the past, one of these was a week-long course in Idaho on snow travel, map reading, route finding, natural shelter construction, site selection, and survival first aid. The second orientation course was a three-day trip from Leadville to Diamond J Ranch over Hagerman Pass, covering the same skills as the first course. Destinations for these courses can vary from year to year.

A course entitled Snow, Ice and Avalanche, taught by the American Avalanche Institute, gives instruction on how to recognize snow stability and how to find routes, and covers backcountry rescue and the use of explosives for avalanche control.

Two courses named Outdoor Leadership are scheduled. One emphasizes interpersonal communication, environmental interpretation, hazard evaluation and decision making. The second is an internship where students take charge of a group and test their new skills.

The Intermediate Telemark Skiing course is a North American Telemark Organization Telemark Workshop and Instructor Training Course. It is taught on intermediate terrain on backcountry nordic equipment.

Two courses called Intermediate Nordic Skiing are given: one is the PSIA Nordic Instructor Clinic to familiarize students with nordic ski instructor requirements; the other is the PSIA Associate Touring Instruction and Tour Leader Instructor Examination.

All these courses are of short duration, usually lasting three to four days. The fee depends on the state and local residency of the student and the course taken. Inquire with the college. All courses provide some college credits.

In the planning stages is a course called Wilderness Time Out, for students who would like to take a rest from school work but would also like to continue earning credits. For about $3,000 per semester, the student combines outdoor experiences, such as mountain climbing, skiing or river rafting, with studies of the flora and fauna and a history of the areas encountered. The fee covers all transportation, room and board, and equipment and instruction.

Contact Jay Zarr, Colorado Mountain College, 3000 114th County Road, Glenwood Springs, Co. 81601, (303) 945-7481. For a catalog describing courses offered at all campus centers in Colorado, send to Colorado Mountain College Administration, 1402 Blake Street, P.O. Box 1001, Glenwood Springs, Co. 81602, (303) 945-8691.

East Divide Lodge

East Divide Lodge, at 8,300 ft., is very isolated, located 10 miles from the nearest telephone and power pole! Visitors to the lodge are met at the road and are guided the 6-1/2 miles to the lodge on a trail maintained by snowmobiles. Access is from Fourmile Park above Glenwood Springs and Ski Sunlight ski area.

Stays at East Divide Lodge are on a reservation basis. The lodge has eight bedrooms and two bathrooms, but no electricity, televisions or telephones. Gourmet meals include steaks, chops, poultry and Oriental cooking. Breakfast, lunch and dinner are served daily to guests at the lodge. Price discounts are given for groups of 15 people. Skiers who drop in may order hot dogs, hamburgers, soups, sandwiches and drinks between noon and 5 p.m.

East Divide Lodge is a destination lodge. After making the long trip to the lodge, and since the return trip is a more difficult uphill climb, skiers generally prefer to stay overnight and ski out the next day.

The trails at East Divide Lodge are moderate in comparison to those of other touring centers mentioned in this book.

There are no maintained trails and no rentals or instruction at East Divide Lodge. Cross-country skiers share the area equally with snowmobilers. The owner, Dennis Yost, hopes to have separate trails to the lodge for snowmobilers and skiers by 1986.

Access: From Interstate 70 take Glenwood Springs-Aspen Exit 116, and pick up Colorado 82 toward Aspen. After two miles, at 23rd Ave. (stoplight), take the right fork (County 117) and follow signs to Ski Sunlight. Take the right fork just before Ski Sunlight to Fourmile Park. Plowed parking is available at the old sawmill before Sunlight Park, or at Fourmile Park. Access is also available from Silt; contact East Divide Lodge for directions from Silt and for detailed directions from the trailheads to the lodge.

Contact Dennis Yost, East Divide Lodge, P.O. Box 1055, Glenwood Springs, Co. 81602, (303) 945-8867.

7W Guest Ranch

Located one hour northwest of Vail in the Flat Tops of the White River National Forest, at 9,000 ft., 7W Guest Ranch is a small family ranch with the capacity to hold 25 people. In the winter, guests may stay in either the lodge or two winterized cabins. Three meals a day, served family style, are included in the package price.

Skiers and snowmobilers share the terrain of packed trails, open plains and flat parks. No rentals are available; instruction can be arranged with advance notice.

Access: From Interstate 70 take Exit 133 and turn left at Sweetwater Creek. Contact Burt George, 7W Guest Ranch, 3412 County Road 150, Gypsum, Co. 81637, (303) 524-9328 for more detailed information and directions.

Sunlight Ski Touring Center

Sunlight Touring Center has maintained trails next to Ski Sunlight ski area since 1979. It is located outside Glenwood Springs, a small resort town 10 miles away. At this writing, the future of the touring center is uncertain.

TRAILS

The trails at Sunlight Touring Center are more to most difficult in comparison to those of other touring centers mentioned in this book.

Sunlight Touring Center has groomed and set 12 km of trails along the base of Compas Mountain, Ski Sunlight's main mountain. The intermediate and advanced trails climb steep hills in parts and eventually reach a beautiful set of meadows and aspen and pine forests which are delightful to ski on. Skiers can leave the trails to telemark down a nearby hill. Fourmile Park, a collection of meadows close to the touring center, is recommended for beginning skiers as it covers flatter terrain. Skiing is free in Fourmile Park.

You can purchase a $5 one-lift lift ticket from Ski Sunlight to use the ski lift. This takes you up Ute Mountain, behind Compas, where you can ski down into the upper meadows of the touring center's trail system. Other trail fees are unknown at this time.

It is not known whether rentals, instruction or guided tours will be available at the touring center.

Races at Sunlight have included: the Gold Dust Classic, the oldest cross-country ski race in Colorado—a 10 km race into the Babbish Gulch area; the Ice Crystal Classic, another 10 km race held in Babbish Gulch during Glenwood Springs' and Sunlight's annual Ski Spree; and the Hot Tub Streak, which entails a five-minute dip in a hot tub and a frolic in the snow.

FOOD AND LODGING

The Sunlight Inn, decorated with a Scandanavian influence and located right at the trailhead, consists of 22 rooms and a large south-facing sundeck with a hot tub. The restaurant serves three meals a day and specializes in continental and traditional American meals. Additional accommodations and restaurants are available in Glenwood Springs. Contact Glenwood Springs Central Reservations; in Colorado, the toll-free number is (800) 221-0098, or the out-of-state number is (303) 945-7295.

ACCESS

From Interstate 70 take Glenwood Springs-Aspen Exit 116, and pick up Colorado 82 toward Aspen. After two miles, at 23rd Ave., take the right fork (just before the stoplight) and follow signs to Ski Sunlight.

Contact Sunlight Touring Center, 10252 County 117, Glenwood Springs, Co. 81601, (303) 945-5225.

Braun Hut System

From Ashcroft townsite.

The Alfred Braun Hut System was developed by the United States Ski Educational Foundation (a non-profit arm of the United States Ski Association (USSA)) with the help of Fred Braun. Originally from Austria, Braun has been a resident of Aspen since 1951 and worked at various jobs before retiring and volunteering his time to the development of the hut system. Under his guidance, five of the huts and the trails leading to them were constructed. One of the six huts had already been refurbished by Stuart Mace, an early dog-sledder in the Ashcroft valley, when Braun started work on them in the mid 1960s. The huts have been in use for over 10 years.

THE HUTS AND THE TRAILS

This hut system is not a chain system. The huts are reached by separate trails and are considered destination huts, though some are accessible to one another. The six huts are located in the Ashcroft area, at 9,500 ft., and all are reached from Ashcroft, an old mining town in which several of the original homes have been restored. The huts are built on National Forest land leased to the USSA.

The huts are equipped with cookstoves, fireplaces, basic cookware, and mattresses. Wood is provided. Drinking water is available from nearby streams or melted snow. There is no electricity and you must provide your own food and sleeping bags.

The Tagert Memorial Hut is located on the Pearl Pass jeep road in the Castle Creek drainage below Castle Peak. One mile away is the Montezuma

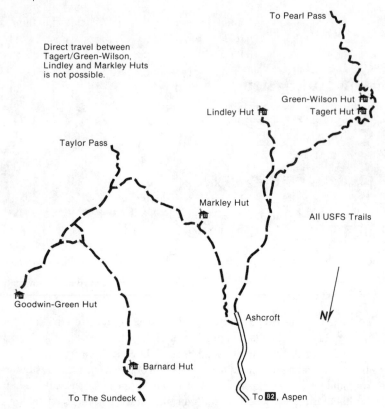

To Pearl Pass

Direct travel between
Tagert/Green-Wilson,
Lindley and Markley Huts
is not possible.

Green-Wilson Hut
Lindley Hut   Tagert Hut

Taylor Pass

Markley Hut

All USFS Trails

Goodwin-Green Hut

Ashcroft

N

Barnard Hut

To The Sundeck   To **82**, Aspen

Mill site. The hut is six miles from Ashcroft at 11,300 ft., an 1,800 ft. elevation gain; there is room for eight people.

The Green Wilson Memorial Hut is located just above the Tagert Hut and is reached by the same trail along the Pearl Pass jeep road. It is also six miles from Ashcroft at 11,350 ft., an 1,850 ft. gain. This hut holds six people.

The Lindley Memorial Hut is located on the Cooper Fork, five miles above Ashcroft. A large hut that holds 18 people, it is situated at 10,600 ft., an 1,100 ft. elevation gain.

The Markley Memorial Hut, on Express Creek, is three miles above Ashcroft on the Taylor Pass road turnoff. Located at 10,200 ft., there is a 700 ft. elevation gain to reach this hut. It is limited to eight people.

The Barnard Memorial Hut is located on the ridge between the Sundeck (the restaurant on top of Aspen Mountain) and Taylor Pass. It is approximately 10 miles from Ashcroft, at 11,600 ft., for an elevation gain of 2,100 ft. This hut is limited to eight people and, because of its remote location, no less than four people are permitted to use it at one time.

The Goodwin-Greene Memorial Hut is in the Gold Hill area, 1-1/2 miles south of Taylor Pass at the head of Difficult Creek. The hut is eight miles from Ashcroft with a 2,000 ft. elevation gain, to 11,500 ft. This hut can hold eight people and, due to its remote location, no less than four people at one time are permitted to use it.

The overnight rate for each hut is $7 per person per night.

Although these trails can be reached without the aid of guides, the huts may be difficult to find, especially in inclement weather. At least one member of each party must be able to read a compass and a map. (These huts are shown on Eagle Eye Maps' Aspen-Carbondale Map; please see the order form in the back of this book.) Skiers should leave Ashcroft before noon to reach the huts in daylight; it is almost impossible to find them in darkness. The USSA assumes no responsibility for the safety of skiers on the trails.

Skiing these backcountry trails is most difficult in comparison to skiing those of other touring centers mentioned in this book, and is entirely different from skiing on prepared tracks. It is recommended that skiers be of at least intermediate ability and that they have some experience in backcountry skiing with a backpack.

There are many avalanche areas along the trails, and Braun or the Forest Service in Aspen, (303) 925-1664, should be consulted as to avalanche dangers before each trip. An avalanche transceiver and safety equipment are recommended.

ACCESS

Ashcroft is located 12 miles from Aspen. From Colorado 82, just west of Aspen, take a right on Maroon Creek Road; take an immediate left at the sign pointing to Ashcroft. Follow this road for 10 miles to a parking area. The Braun hut trails begin on the two Forest Service roads at the parking area. Ashcroft Ski Touring Unlimited is located at this point; you are asked to stay on the public roads.

All reservations are made through Mr. Fred Braun at 702 W. Main Street, Aspen, Co. 81611, (303) 925-7162. Follow Colorado 82 into Aspen. His office is on the northwest corner of Colorado 82 (or Main St.) and Sixth St.

Tenth Mountain Trail Association

The Tenth Mountain Trail Association is a non-profit organization that has created one of the finest hut systems in the United States. It was started by Aspen architect Fritz Benedict, a member of the Tenth Mountain Division during World War II which trained in the mountains of Colorado (mainly at Camp Hale near Leadville, though they trained all over the Colorado Rockies) to help fight the war in the Alps of Europe. Some of these men returned to Colorado to build the ski resorts in the state, including both Aspen and Vail. Benedict thought the trail should be a memorial to men of the famous alpine troops who had done so much to build the sport of skiing throughout the country.

Benedict skied the Haute Route in Europe, from Chamonix to Zermatt; his ideas for the Tenth Mountain Trail were inspired by the European hut system. In 1980 he began working with the Forest Service to select routes and locations for the huts; an Environmental Assessment was completed. He then formed his group, originally the Western Slope Trail Association and now the Tenth Mountain Trail Association, which directed the work and fund raising.

In planning the trail, avalanche areas were avoided and the hut locations were chosen to be only seven to 10 miles apart, so that the trail would be suitable for intermediate skiers. Existing ski ranches were incorporated into the route to save money on huts and to provide a variety of settings for the skiers to visit.

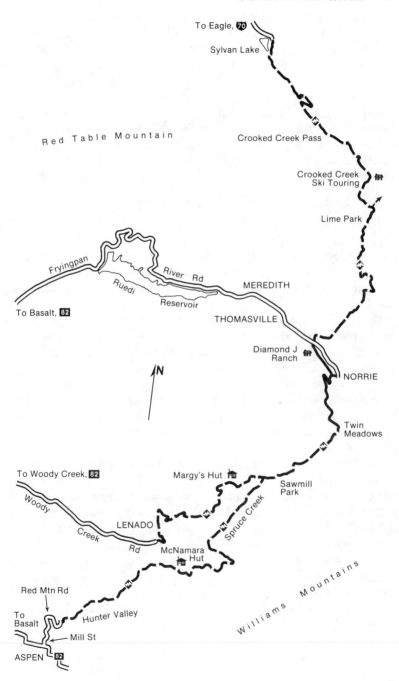

At the same time, Robert S. McNamara, former Secretary of State, and Dr. Ben Eiseman were raising money to finance the construction of the first two huts. They were to be dedicated in memory of McNamara's wife, Margaret McNamara, who had enjoyed skiing in the mountains. The two huts were built in the summer of 1982, completing the first part of the Tenth Mountain Trail.

The remaining six huts are still in the planning stages. As of this writing, the Forest Service is working on an Environmental Assessment, and it is hoped that the Tenth Mountain Trail Association will be able to build additional huts this summer (1985) and in the summer of 1986. The trail, when completed, will cover 80 miles of Rocky Mountain terrain from Aspen to Vail.

THE TRAIL AND THE HUTS

The trail begins two miles from Aspen on Hunter Creek Road at an elevation of 8,300 ft. This section of the trail, the least difficult, climbs 2,180 ft. and covers six miles to the first hut, McNamara Hut, at 10,480 ft. The location affords spectacular views of the Elk Mountains, the Maroon Bells and Aspen.

The next hut, Margy's Hut, is eight miles from McNamara Hut, at first an 800 ft. drop and then a 1,700 ft. climb, ending at 11,300 ft. This is the most difficult section, following a narrow hiking trail. An alternate access to Margy's Hut starts at Lenado, and continues over a seven-mile, four-wheel-drive road with a steady 2,600 ft. climb. Margy's Hut is located above the Spruce Creek drainage and overlooks the Williams Mountains. The peak of Mount Yeckel, 11,765 ft. high, is nearby and can be climbed and telemarked; the view at the top encompasses the Holy Cross Wilderness, the Elk Range and Red Table Mountain.

From Margy's Hut, the trail continues for 10 miles to Diamond J Ranch, dropping 2,900 ft. to 8,250 ft. The first five miles of this section are more difficult, following an occasionally steep, narrow hiking trail. Diamond J, a ranch operated by the Sims family, offers lodging and meals.

From Diamond J, skiers can leave the trail or ski farther to Crooked Creek, eight miles up Lime Creek and a 1,150 ft. elevation gain to 9,500 ft.

Margy's and McNamara huts are rustic, backcountry cabins. They are stocked with firewood and wood-burning stoves, cookware and dishes, mattresses and pillows, lanterns, garbage bags, matches, paper towels, toilet paper, and kitchen supplies. There is no water or electricity. Each of the huts holds 15 people.

Tenth Mountain Trail charges $12 per person per night for each cabin. If a party contains less than 15 people, the cabin may include other groups.

In general, the trails are not marked, though blue diamonds help distinguish them when trail-finding could be confusing. Skiers cannot depend on these markers; map and compass reading skills are necessary for skiing this trail. (Eagle Eye Maps' Aspen/Carbondale Cross Country Ski Map shows the trail from Aspen to Crooked Creek. See the order form in the back of this book.)

The Tenth Mountain Trail can be skied without guides, although groups without backcountry skiing experience are encouraged to hire a guide to help locate trails or to ease the burden of finding the huts in inclement weather. Suggested guide services are Crooked Creek Ski Touring (which guides skiers from Crooked Creek to Aspen) at P.O. Box 3142, Vail, Co. 81658, (303) 949-5682; and Rocky Mountain Climbing School/Aspen Touring Center, P.O. Box 2432, Aspen, Co. 81612, (303) 925-7625. These are qualified guides familiar with the Tenth Mountain Trail, as well as with weather and snow conditions and avalanche areas and dangers. Guides can also provide instruction on backcountry and telemark techniques.

The Tenth Mountain Trail is rated more difficult to most difficult in comparison to trails at the touring centers mentioned in this book. It is emphasized that the trail was designed for the intermediate skier and that some sections may require advanced techniques. Tenth Mountain Trail Association stresses that beginners not attempt this trail. Skiers must be able to break trail in deep snow with a heavy pack on their backs. The weather changes quickly in the mountains and can turn a challenging trip into a difficult fight for survival. Skiers must be able to read topographic maps and use a compass, have an awareness of avalanche dangers, and know rescue and emergency medical techniques.

To help plan your trip, you are given a backcountry safety handout which outlines trip planning, equipment that should be taken, and backcountry safety techniques. A general reference map and a list of topographic maps necessary for the trip are provided.

RESERVATION INFORMATION

The Tenth Mountain Trail accepts reservations for the two huts only. Contact Tenth Mountain Trail Association, 1280 Ute Ave., Aspen, Co. 81611, (303) 925-5775. Separate reservations must be made with Diamond J, 26604 Fryingpan Road, Meredith, Co. 81642, (303) 927-3222, and Crooked Creek (see above address) for the use of their facilities.

ACCESS

In Aspen, from the intersection of Mill and Main Streets at the Hotel Jerome, drive north on Mill St. past Clark's Market and the post office. Cross the Roaring Fork River at 1/4 mile and bear left on Red Mountain Road. Cross Hunter Creek at a half mile, then climb steeply to a short, level section of road followed by a steep right turn in the road at 1 mile. At 1-1/2 miles, when Red Mountain Road switches back to the left, turn right and downhill onto Hunter Creek Road. Follow this road for another 1/4 mile to the Private Road entrance, where a road climbs steeply to the left past a house and a water tank. Proceed another 300 feet to the parking area. To reach the trailhead, walk back to the Hunter Creek Road, then uphill .3 mile to the trail's beginning.

Contact Elizabeth Holekamp or Rob Burnett, Tenth Mountain Trail Association, 1280 Ute Ave., Aspen, Co. 81611, (303) 925-5775.

At Bear Pole Ranch.

Aspen Touring Center

Dick Jackson started the Rocky Mountain Climbing School/Aspen Touring Center in 1976. A climbing and ski-mountaineering enthusiast since the late 1960s, he is concerned with helping the interested learner become accustomed to outdoor recreation all year round. In the summer, the climbing school offers courses in rock climbing, snow climbing, and backcountry awareness, with expeditions to New Zealand, Europe and South America. In the winter, Aspen Touring Center is involved with cross-country skiing.

"The Trolley" in Aspen is the meeting point for all tours handled by the Aspen Touring Center. Rentals are available at the Trolley and the cost is included in the tour price. There are 20 pairs of skis available—some touring, some metal-edged, about one-half waxless, and one-half waxable skis.

Jackson instructs beginner skiers on the 70 km of trails maintained by the Aspen/Snowmass Nordic Council. He uses Forest Service backcountry trails and the Tenth Mountain Trail for more advanced skiers and for courses in ski-mountaineering.

INSTRUCTION AND FEES

Aspen Touring Center employs six to eight part-time instructors for teaching and touring. All the instructors are PSIA-certified; Aspen Touring Center is a PSIA-certified school. Jackson believes in keeping his student/guide ratio low so that all students are guaranteed personal attention and maximum participation. Beginning to intermediate track lessons are given on the Aspen Golf Course daily from 10 a.m. to noon. The cost is $20 per person.

Telemark and downhill cross-country instruction is conducted in both private and group lessons using the facilities at Buttermilk Ski Area. Downhill techniques can be taught in backcountry conditions. The price depends on the class taken.

Full-day ski tours are scheduled daily; a minimum of three persons must attend. The backcountry-trail tours include treks to Independence Pass, Owl Creek Trail, Hunter Creek, and Government Trail, to name a few. Lessons in backcountry technique are included. Tours are scheduled from 10 a.m. to 3:30 p.m. and can include prepared lunches if there are more than four people per tour. The cost for a private tour is $120 per day, three persons cost $40 each, four or more cost $30 each. Half-day tours are also available, scheduled by reservation only. The price for a private tour is $65, a three-person class costs $25 per person, and four or more people cost $20 per person.

Guide service is offered for the Tenth Mountain Trail Hut System and the Fred Braun Hut System as well as for a tour from Aspen to Crested Butte. Aspen Touring Center reserves the Tenth Mountain Trail huts for several dates each winter and takes reservations for these dates. Guides take groups from Aspen to the McNamara Hut the first night; the second and third nights are spent at Margy's Hut; and the last night is spent at Diamond J Ranch. Small groups are taken; Jackson tries not to schedule more than six people per tour. The cost, including transportation, food, lodging and guide service, is $250 per person.

The Aspen-to-Crested Butte tour includes skiing from Ashcroft over Pearl Pass in terrain well above timberline and is considered more difficult than the Tenth Mountain Trail. The trip includes an overnight stay in one of the Braun huts, either the Tagert or the Wilson hut, six miles from the starting point. The next night is spent in the Friends' Hut, or in a snow cave built by Jackson, near the top of Pearl Pass, at 12,400 ft., four miles from the two Braun huts. From Pearl Pass to Crested Butte is a distance of 10 miles. This trip includes a chartered flight from Crested Butte back to Aspen. The cost, including the flight, food, lodging and guide service, is $210.

Special tours and moonlight tours are available on request. Inquire at Aspen Touring Center.

OTHER OFFERINGS

Ski-Mountaineering (or Ski Randonee) tours are offered on a regular basis depending on weather and existing snow conditions. Since these tours are taken in the spring after lifts have closed, skiers must climb the mountain by themselves. Alpine-touring or metal-edged skis, along with climbing skins and wax, aid in the climb. Some areas visited on this tour are Mount Sopris and Hayden Peak.

A Spring Mountain Guide Training Seminar is taught through the Rocky Mountain Climbing School/Aspen Touring Center for those interested in guiding professionally. Though no certification is awarded after this course, students benefit from the extensive experience of the instructors. Topics covered are snow and rock climbing, avalanche awareness, route finding, mountain medical emergencies, backcountry ski technique and expedition planning, with lectures and video and slide presentations. The seminar, given once a year in spring, lasts for five days, and maintains a four-to-one student-to-guide ratio. The cost is $325 per person.

ACCESS

The Trolley car is located in Aspen at Rubey Park, at the corner of Galena and Durant Streets. Contact Dick Jackson, Aspen Touring Center, P.O. Box 2432, Aspen, Co. 81612, (303) 925-7625.

Colorado First Tracks

Colorado First Tracks has been in operation since 1976, with United States Forest Service permits for the Elk Mountains between Crested Butte and Marble. Flying to elevations as high as 13,200 ft., vertical descents of 2,000 to 4,000 ft. are possible.

The heliport, where orientation procedures take place, is located in Marble. Van service from Aspen airport and the Amtrak station in Glenwood Springs is provided by the Redstone Inn in Redstone. The heliport is only a 15-minute ride from the Redstone Inn.

Colorado First Tracks' season generally runs from February 1 to March 31. Tours are mostly alpine in nature with an emphasis on vertical drops, though nordic tours can be arranged. These nordic tours include a helicopter ride up into the mountains, skiing in alpine meadows, lunch, and a flight down. Guides are happy to instruct skiers in telemarking, if the entire group is agreeable.

Group size is limited to seven clients and one guide. A day of skiing runs $245 for a guaranteed 10,000-vertical-foot ski day. Price includes trail mix, fruit, juice and hot soup. A 10% discount is given for an organizer of a group of seven. Additional runs can be purchased for $15 per 1,000 vertical feet.

Colorado First Tracks' guides are experienced downhill nordic skiers trained in first aid and in backcountry avalanche prediction. Clients should be intermediate or advanced skiers. Colorado First Tracks can help make rental arrangements through local ski stores.

Contact: Murray Cunningham, Colorado First Tracks, P.O. Box 9558, Aspen, Co. 81612, (303) 925-7735.

Backcountry Trails

Carbondale area: Fourmile Park* (E); Chapman Campground* (E); North Fork* (E); Cunningham Creek* (E); Hagerman Pass Road* (EM); Fourmile Road* (M); McClure Pass* (M); Bogan Flats* (M); Dinkle Lake* (M); Thomas Lakes* (M); Avalanche Creek* (M); Marion Gulch (M); Lime Park* (MD); Tenth Mountain Trail* (D).

The Sopris Ranger District—White River NF, 620 Main, Carbondale, 81623, 963-2266—administers the above.

Aspen area: Ashcroft Road* (E); Difficult Campground* (E); Highway 82* (M); Hunter Valley* (M); Snowmass Creek* (M); Government Trail* (M); Tenth Mountain Trail* (D); Braun Hut System trails* (D); Hay Park (D); Williams Lake (D). Several popular trails around Aspen are discouraged due to extreme avalanche danger. These are the Maroon Bells Road, Conun-drum Hot Springs Trail and Pearl Pass Road.

The Aspen Ranger District—White River NF, 806 W. Hallam, Aspen, 81611, 925-3445—administers the above.

* Shown on Eagle Eye's ASPEN-CARBONDALE map.

(E) Easier, (M) Moderate, (D) Difficult.

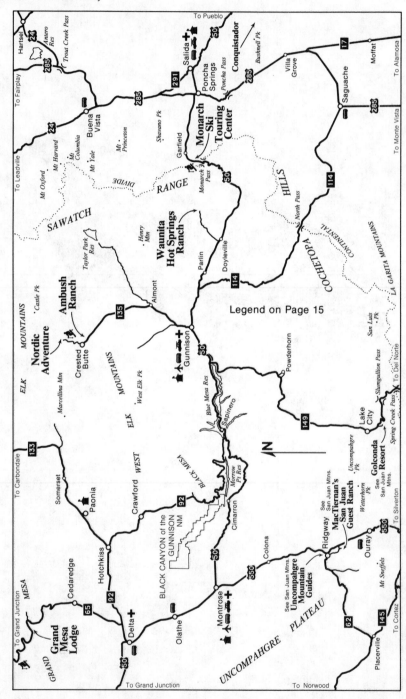

Legend on Page 15

Gunnison Valley

The Gunnison geographic section covers a widespread area of west-central Colorado. Starting in the southeasternmost part of the Gunnison section is the Conquistador ski area, located outside Westcliffe south of Canon City. Conquistador is located in the San Isabel National Forest in the Sangre de Cristo Mountains. Northwest of Conquistador is Monarch Pass, at the top of which the Monarch Ski Touring Center is located, alongside U.S. 50. Following U.S. 50 westward, you come to the Waunita Hot Springs Ranch, about 25 miles east of Gunnison. North of Gunnison, in the Crested Butte area, are Ambush Ranch and the Nordic Adventure/Trak Ski Touring Center. Then, distant but still in the Gunnison region, is Grand Mesa Lodge, located at the top of Grand Mesa about 125 miles to the northwest.

This part of the Gunnison River Valley is covered by the Gunnison, San Isabel and the Grand Mesa national forests; it is surrounded by the Cochetopa Hills and the Sawatch Range to the east, the Uncompahgre Mountains to the south, the West Elk Mountains in the northern section and Grand Mesa to the west. In the middle of all this is the Blue Mesa Reservoir, which is surrounded by the Curecanti National Recreation Area, popular for fishing, boating, water sports and camping in the summer. The reservoir, combined with the Morrow Point and Crystal reservoirs, makes up a large water storage project. At the westernmost tip of these reservoirs is the Black Canyon of the Gunnison, one of the deepest canyons in the United States.

This section of western Colorado is supported by the mining of gold, coal and ore in Crested Butte, on Monarch Pass and in the North Fork Valley of the Gunnison, and ranching in the entire region. Visitors are attracted by hunting in the fall and fishing, hiking and camping in the summer. The area's four downhill ski resorts are Conquistador, Monarch, Crested Butte, and Powderhorn on Grand Mesa.

Cross-country skiing is basically in its developmental stage, though Ambush Ranch and Nordic Adventure have been around for several years. Backcountry ski trails abound and have been the most popular aspect of the sport for many years.

Access depends on your destination. A variety of airlines serve airports in Gunnison, Montrose and Grand Junction. Continental Trailways buses serve Gunnison, Salida, Montrose, and Grand Junction. U.S. 50, from Pueblo to the east to Grand Junction to the west, passes through the heart of this region, through Gunnison and over Monarch Pass.

Ambush Ranch

Ambush Ranch is run by Steve Rieschl, former captain of the 1962 World Championship Ski Team, exemplar of the book, "Steve Rieschl's Ski Touring For The Fun Of It," (published by Sports Illustrated), and skier for over 43 years. Rieschl looked for five years to find an area in the western United States that would make an outstanding nordic touring center. He chose the Crested Butte area because of the excellent cross-country terrain and its beauty. Crested Butte is an old mining town in the Elk Mountains; Crested Butte Mountain is the alpine ski mountain and Mt. Crested Butte is the downhill resort town located two miles north of Crested Butte.

The touring center was first run from a lodge in Crested Butte. Skiers were shuttled to the original Ambush Ranch, a cabin located on 140 acres behind Crested Butte Mountain, surrounded on three sides by National Forest. This ranch is now used by skiers as a destination for lunch or for overnight trips. The touring center presently operates from Skyland Resort, a complex including a golf club, an athletic facility, a restaurant, lounge and condominiums. A track system is maintained there and offers a new dimension to Ambush Ranch, adding groomed trails to the original backcountry program.

Other winter activities in the area include downhill skiing on Crested Butte Mountain, and swimming, jacuzzi, racquetball, indoor tennis, and an athletic club with a weight room, all available at Skyland Resort.

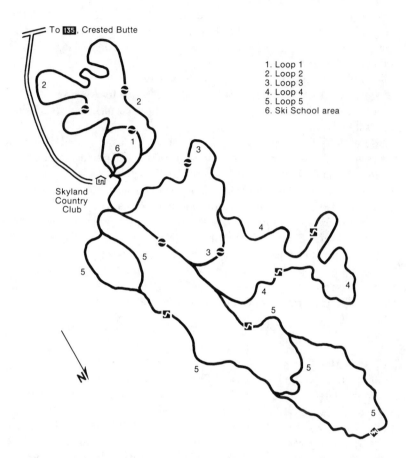

To **135**, Crested Butte

1. Loop 1
2. Loop 2
3. Loop 3
4. Loop 4
5. Loop 5
6. Ski School area

Skyland
Country
Club

N

TRAILS

The Ambush Ranch trails at Skyland Ranch are rated moderate in comparison to those of other touring centers mentioned in this book.

Rieschl maintains 10 to 15 km of trails at Skyland Resort, mostly double-tracked except on advanced terrain. The majority are intermediate trails; one is easy, and one advanced. In 1985, the trails were maintained only on the golf course, but plans include new trails on the lower part of Crested Butte Mountain by 1986 (see trail map).

A trail pass costs $3; a half-day trail pass is $2; a three-day pass is $8; and children under seven ski for free. A season pass for an individual costs $50; the family rate is $135. Trails are open daily from 9 a.m. to 4 p.m.

RENTALS AND INSTRUCTION

Sixty pairs of Fischer skis are available to rent from the ski shop in the Skyland clubhouse. All have the Salomon Nordic boot and binding system. Though mostly touring skis, some are demonstration-racing, touring skis and telemarking skis.

The full-day rental fee for a complete set is $9; half-day rental for a full set costs $6.50; children's rentals cost $6. Three- and five-day rental rates are available. Telemark skis are $10 per day; high-performance demo skis are $13.

Instruction is available for all levels of skiing from introductory to advanced. Telemarking, cross-country downhill, and racing classes are taught. Ambush Ranch is a PSIA-certified ski school; Rieschl is a PSIA instructor and examiner and trains his own instructors. All instructors are either certified by PSIA or are working on certification.

Telemarking can be taught on Crested Butte Mountain or on many suitable slopes in the Crested Butte area.

Lessons are scheduled at 10 a.m. and 1:30 p.m. daily and require one-day advance notice. All lessons cost $14, a lesson and tour cost $20, and private lessons are available at $35 per hour, or $140 per day for one to six people. Group rates are available. All of the above rates include a trail pass.

GUIDED TOURS

Guided tour possibilities around Crested Butte are unlimited. The first and most popular is a trip to the log cabin at Ambush Ranch. The cabin is a two-mile, almost-level ski from the trailhead, to which skiers are transported from Skyland. The cabin is furnished with comfortable beds, gas stove, gas refrigerator, woodstove, and sundeck. It is available for overnight stays and sleeps up to eight people. Beginner to advanced skiing terrain can be found near the cabin.

Group rates for a two-person minimum, with a guide, is $35 per person per night. Private use of the cabin costs $105 per night with a $20 charge per person for the guide fee. There is an additional charge for meals.

For interested parties, over 138 miles of touring terrain through the surrounding river valleys are available. Group tours cost $20 per person for a full day, or $14 for a half day. A cabin at Elkton, a six-mile trip on intermediate terrain that starts at 9,200 ft. and ends at 10,400 ft., is used as a destination. Overnight snow-camping trips as well as guided tours from Crested Butte to Aspen over Pearl Pass are also available. The Friends' Hut is used for overnights for this trip. Prices vary according to arrangements.

Skiers either provide their own meals or may receive them for an extra charge on all tours.

RACES AND SPECIAL EVENTS
One race, part of a Crested Butte cross-country race series, is held in February. Group ski touring and Christian presentations are held for three days in April and include Christian lectures and discussions combined with cross-country skiing. Inquire at Ambush Ranch for rates and schedule.

FOOD AND LODGING
A restaurant, open for dinner, and a snack bar, open for lunch and snacks, are located at Skyland Resort. Condominiums adjacent to the touring center are available to rent. Other lodging and restaurants can be found in Crested Butte and Mt. Crested Butte. Contact Crested Butte Central Reservations, Mt. Crested Butte, Co. 81225. Local telephone, (303) 349-2222; Colorado toll-free (800) 332-5875; out-of-state toll-free, (800) 525-4220.

ACCESS
Located 26 miles north of Gunnison and two miles south of Crested Butte, Ambush Ranch is located just off Colorado 135 at Skyland Resort. American Airlines and Trans-Colorado Airlines serve Gunnison from Denver. Continental Trailways bus serves Gunnison from both the east and the west. There is free shuttle service from Crested Butte to Skyland and the touring center.

Contact Steve Rieschl or Bob Bernard, Ambush Ranch, P.O. Box 1230-GS, Crested Butte, Co. 81224, (303) 349-5408 or (303) 349-6131.

Monarch Ski Touring Center

Monarch Ski Touring Center is located close to the Monarch Pass summit, at 10,000 ft., between Salida and Gunnison. The center itself is located on top of the Madonna Mine, an old silver and gold mine. Second only to Wolf Creek Pass, the Monarch Pass area receives the highest average snowfall in Colorado. The average is 300 inches of snow per year.

The touring center is owned and run by Alex Menard, who leases the land from Monarch Ski Area. Menard has skied in Aspen for years and recently maintained a trail system in Leadville.

Menard hopes his is the first touring center to open each year on the first of November, and plans to have a hot tub and sauna at the touring center by 1986 to offer visitors after a hard day of skiing.

TRAILS

The trails at Monarch Ski Touring Center are moderate in comparison to those of other touring centers mentioned in this book.

Menard maintains 10 to 15 km of cross-country trails—80% of them beginner, 15% intermediate, and 5% advanced. These trails are double-tracked, well marked by blue diamonds, and they wind through the Monarch Park area along the South Arkansas River.

There is no access to backcountry skiing from the trails because of extreme avalanche danger in the surrounding area. Please heed avalanche warning signs.

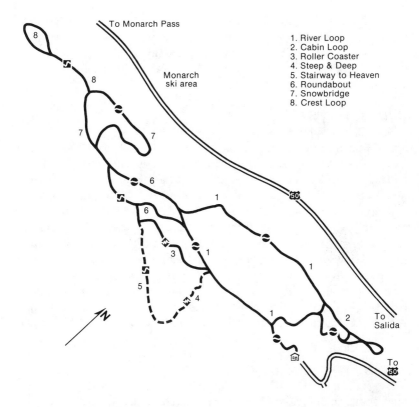

1. River Loop
2. Cabin Loop
3. Roller Coaster
4. Steep & Deep
5. Stairway to Heaven
6. Roundabout
7. Snowbridge
8. Crest Loop

Excellent areas for deep-powder telemarking are on the slopes connecting the Stairway to Heaven and the Roller Coaster trails.

The trail fee is $3 a day, $10 per family, and includes waxing, warming hut and free hot drinks. The center is open daily from 10 a.m. to 4 p.m.

RENTALS AND INSTRUCTION

The touring center at Monarch has 30 pairs of waxless Karhu touring skis for rent. All have the Trak Contact binding system. Karhu and Kazama telemark skis are available. The center is capable of outfitting young children and has skins, sleds and shovels to rent for backcountry touring.

A complete track set for adults rents for $7, children's skis are $5. A complete telemark set is $12.

Instruction is provided by three instructors; Menard is certified by PSIA. Lessons are offered for beginners through racing and telemarking. Telemarking is taught at Monarch Ski Area. Lessons are scheduled daily at 10:30 a.m. and 12:30 p.m. Half-day, full-day and private lessons are offered.

Half-day private lessons are $20 and half-day group lessons are $10. Full-day private lessons are $30, full-day group lessons are $15. The Telemark Package includes a half-day lesson, complete ski rental and a full-day lift ticket at Monarch, for $25. The Track Package includes a half-day lesson with ski rental and trail pass for $18.

GUIDED TOURS

Several guided tours are offered. The half-day Crest Tour starts at the top of Monarch Pass and returns to Monarch Ski Touring Center. The Fooses Creek Tour begins at Monarch Pass; skiers then cross a ridge and telemark downhill for nine miles. Another tour is guided on the Old Monarch Pass Road, which provides scenic views of the Colorado Rockies.

Overnight tours are available. A tour up Middle Creek Valley to a cabin near Mt. Aetna has a 1,000 ft. elevation gain. A two-night tour crosses Chalk Creek Pass to the ghost town of St. Elmo and ends with a dip in the Mt. Princeton Hot Springs. Skiing in this area can be dangerous because of frequent avalanches; guides are recommended for your safety.

Overnight cabin tours, including a guide, three meals a day and ski rental, cost $75 per day. A half day costs $20 for a private tour and $10 per person for a group tour. Full-day private tours cost $30 and $15 per person for a group tour.

RACES AND SPECIAL EVENTS

Menard hopes to have a series of four citizens' races starting in 1986, one per month from December through March. Each event will be a different type of race. Four free racing clinics will be held prior to the monthly races. These clinics will be heavily structured half days covering racing skills—training, waxing, course topography and ski techniques. As of this writing, only one event was held in 1985, consisting of 7.5 and 15 km races.

FOOD AND LODGING

Monarch Ski Touring Center is located two miles from Garfield, where there are restaurants and accommodations. Gunnison, 40 miles west, and Salida, 24 miles east, offer a larger variety of both. Menard, experienced in food service as well as skiing, will have a small restaurant at the touring center by 1986 offering healthy lunch fare.

ACCESS

Monarch Ski Touring Center is located five miles east of the top of Monarch Pass on U.S. 50 between Salida and Gunnison.

Contact Alex Menard, Monarch Ski Touring Center, Garfield, Co. 81227, (303) 539-3816; or toll-free, (800) 332-3668.

Nordic Adventure/Trak Ski Touring Center

Nordic Adventure, associated with the alpine resort at Mt. Crested Butte, was begun in 1977 with Rick Borkovec acting as director. One of the first to re-introduce telemark skiing to the sport of cross-country skiing, Borkovec has taught and coached many telemark clinics in the United States. He is a PSIA-certified ski touring guide and examiner.

In 1979, Trak began sponsoring the touring center and helped set up the ski rental program. The touring center operates its rentals and lessons from the ski lodge in the Gothic Building, at the base of the ski lifts.

TRAILS

The trails at Nordic Adventure are rated easier to moderate in comparison to those of other touring centers mentioned in this book.

Beginning at 9,200 ft., the trails are set 1.5 miles down the road from the rental shop toward the town of Gothic. Shuttle service is provided by the touring center for visitors who rent skis and sign up for lessons. Skiers using the trails but not taking lessons can board the shuttle if there is room; otherwise they must provide their own transportation. Adequate parking is available at the stables located near the trailhead.

Thirteen kilometers of trails are maintained and marked. Half are beginner trails, 20% are intermediate and 30% are advanced. All are double-tracked and cross exposed pasture land. The touring center is open from 8:30 a.m. to 4:30 p.m. and there is no trail fee.

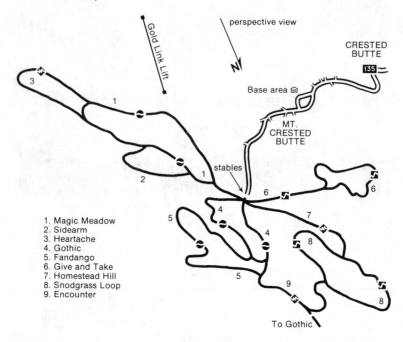

1. Magic Meadow
2. Sidearm
3. Heartache
4. Gothic
5. Fandango
6. Give and Take
7. Homestead Hill
8. Snodgrass Loop
9. Encounter

One backcountry trail is accessible from the trail system. The road to Gothic extends from the Encounter Trail and continues 3.5 miles to the town. This trail is sometimes closed due to avalanche danger; skiers must check avalanche conditions before attempting to use the trail.

RENTALS AND INSTRUCTION

There are 120 pairs of Trak and Kneissl skis, with Trak Contact bindings, available to rent. Half of these are touring skis, the other half are telemark skis. The touring skis are mostly waxless, though waxable skis are available. Children as young as four years old can be outfitted.

A full adult set costs $9 for a full day, $6 for a half day; a full children's set is $6 for a full day, $4 for a half day. High-performance demonstration skis, top-line telemark and racing skis and boots can be rented for $12 for a full day, $8 for a half day.

Nordic Adventure is a PSIA-certified ski school. The six instructors are also certified with PSIA. All levels of touring are taught as well as racing and telemark skiing. Touring instruction takes place on the trails. This ski school specializes in telemark instruction, generally on Mt. Crested Butte, though backcountry telemarking lessons can be taught. Skiers taking beginning telemark lessons at Mt. Crested Butte do not have to pay for the lift ticket.

A half-day group lesson is $14 for adults, $8 for children. A full-day group lesson for an adult is $22 and $12 for children. Private lessons are $35 for the first hour, $45 for two hours, $55 for three hours; each additional person costs $10.

Two track and telemark skiing clinics are held each year and include an all-morning coaching session. The track skiing clinic teaches the diagonal stride, double poling, the marathon skate, and the skate turn and tuck. The telemark clinic covers all levels from easy terrain to bumps, crud and powder. Each clinic is two hours long and costs $6.

The multi-day lift tickets sold at Mt. Crested Butte are exchangeable at Nordic Adventure for touring activities. The value of the ticket is $17 and can be exchanged for rentals and lessons.

GUIDED TOURS

Day tours cover several areas in the Elk Mountains. Half- and full-day tours are available. Washington Gulch, and the Brush Creek, East River, Slate River and Coal Creek valleys can all be toured.

Other tours offered include overnight trips in which skiers stay in a mountain hut or learn to make snow caves; moonlight tours with hot wine; and tours to Aspen over Pearl Pass with an overnight stay at Friends' Hut. Elkton, a ghost town 10 miles from Crested Butte, is another destination for an overnight tour and can be skied by a beginner. There are tours available for skiers of all abilities.

A full-day tour is $22; a half-day tour is $14; a morning lesson with an afternoon tour is $22; the moonlight tour costs $15; an overnight trip to Aspen is $135 (2 days, one night, meals included); other overnights are $75 per person per night. A minimum of three people for each overnight trip is necessary.

RACES AND SPECIAL EVENTS

Nordic Adventure sponsors several races each year on its own trails and elsewhere. The first race of the year, in December, is a seven-mile trip from the stables parking lot to Gothic and back. The Trak Team Challenge is a relay race and takes place in January; in this race, there are four people to a team, and at least one team member must be a woman.

Two events are memorial races named for local skiers. Al Johnson was a mail carrier in the area who skied his mail deliveries in the winter. He was also a top racer who won a local race for several consecutive years until beaten by Charlie Baney. Charlie's race is a 20 km race and Al's race is an uphill-downhill race. Both are held in March.

The North American Telemark Championships and the National Qualifying Races are held in March.

FOOD AND LODGING

Mt. Crested Butte boasts 6,000 beds for visitors, and there is lodging in the historic town of Crested Butte. There are numerous restaurants in each town. Contact Crested Butte Central Reservations, Mt. Crested Butte, Co. 81225. Local telephone, (303) 349-2222; Colorado toll-free (800) 332-5875; out-of-state toll-free, (800) 525-4220.

ACCESS

Crested Butte is 28 miles north of Gunnison, which is served by Continental Trailways bus, American Airlines and Trans-Colorado Airlines from Denver. The Gothic Building is located in Mt. Crested Butte, about two miles north of Crested Butte.

Contact Rick Borkovec, Nordic Adventure/Trak Ski Touring Center, Box A, Mt. Crested Butte, Co. 81225, (303) 349-2250.

Grand Mesa Lodge

If you like to ski in uncrowded situations, with unlimited amounts of powder from November to May, then Grand Mesa Lodge is for you. Grand Mesa is an enormous flat-topped mountain, the largest in the world, covered with 300 to 400 feet of lava from ancient volcanos. Its elevation is over 10,000 feet; snow depth averages nine or 10 feet a year. From the south side you can see the Elk, the San Juan and the Uncompahgre mountain ranges and the semi-arid plains leading into Utah; to the north you can see toward Grand Junction and miles and miles of the flat-topped mesas of oil shale country. The top of the mesa consists of rolling hills, meadows and pine forests, and is spotted with 300 lakes. Grand Mesa Lodge sits on the southern edge of Grand Mesa.

Bob and Linda Hickman have owned and run the lodge since 1982. John Burritt, a former Olympic skier, assisted the Hickmans in designing and creating the trails.

TRAILS

The trails at Grand Mesa Lodge are rated easier to moderate in comparison to those of other touring centers mentioned in this book.

Twelve kilometers of beginner and intermediate trails are maintained just across Colorado 65 from the lodge. They are mostly double-tracked; in heavily used areas three or four tracks are set. Because of location, backcountry skiing is difficult from the trails, though some backcountry trails are situated not far from the lodge.

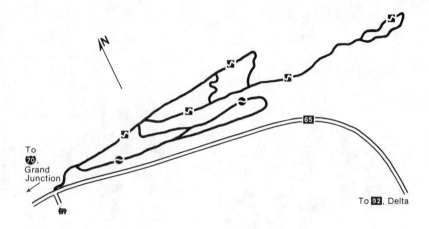

Several areas of Grand Mesa lend themselves to telemarking and cross-country downhill skiing. On the entire mesa, backcountry skiing is limited only by certain areas reserved for snowmobiles. Miles and miles of relatively avalanche-free terrain are just right for making tracks in fluffy powder.

The trail fee at Grand Mesa Lodge is $2 per person, or $5 per carload. The touring center is open from 9 a.m. to 4 p.m.

RENTALS AND INSTRUCTION

Fifty pairs of mostly Trak waxless touring skis are available to rent. Children can be outfitted; some of the children's skis are old, wide downhill skis fitted with cross-country bindings.

Rental rates for adults are $7.50 for a full set for a full day, or $6 for a full set for a half day. Full sets for children are $5 for a full or half day. Groups of 10 or more receive 10% off rentals plus 5% off for six or more consecutive days of skiing. The multiple-day rate for six or more consecutive days includes 10% off rentals.

Lessons are provided by a number of local skiers. John Burritt and his son, Brad, teach basic and advanced skiing. Bob Hickman can also instruct. Telemark lessons are available. Groups of four are charged $8 per hour; a group of eight is charged $16 per hour, and so on. Reservations for lessons are required 48 hours in advance.

FOOD AND LODGING

There is a small restaurant-lounge at Grand Mesa Lodge which prepares American and Mexican dinners by reservation only. Hot snacks are served during the day without reservations.

Accommodations include 14 cabins, not all of which are open during the winter, nestled within the spruce forest surrounding the lodge. All are equipped with kitchens, bathrooms with showers, and woodstoves, and they hold up to six people. Wood is provided. Rates are $20 per cabin.

ACCESS

Grand Mesa Lodge is located 18 miles north of Cedaredge and 55 miles southeast of Grand Junction on Colorado 65. Airlines, Amtrak, and Continental Trailways buses serve Grand Junction.

Contact Bob and Linda Hickman, Grand Mesa Lodge, Star Route 205, Cedaredge, Co. 81413, (303) 856-3211.

Trails on top of Grand Mesa.

Waunita Hot Springs Ranch

Waunita Hot Springs Ranch, at 8,946 ft., is named for the abundant natural hot springs that bubble up on the ranch property. It is located about 25 miles east of Gunnison and borders the Gunnison National Forest. Owned for 23 years by Rod and Junelle Pringle and family, it has been run for years as a dude ranch during the summer. The original hotel, built in 1880, was destroyed by a fire in 1910. The present lodge was built in 1915 when Waunita was a health resort featuring mud packs and soaks in the hot springs. In the 1950s the ranch was a baseball camp for aspiring youngsters and remained so until the Pringles purchased it in 1962.

The hot springs provide enough hot water to heat the whole ranch and to fill the 35 ft. by 90 ft. swimming pool. The pool can be lighted for night swimming.

The ranch was open during the winter season mainly for church and youth groups until, in the winter of 1984-85, the Pringles decided to offer a cross-country skiing program and to accommodate smaller groups and individuals as well.

Waunita Hot Springs Ranch is a member of the Colorado Cross Country Ski Association.

TRAILS

The skiing at Waunita Hot Springs Ranch is moderate in comparison to that of other touring centers mentioned in this book.

Although generally not maintained, trails can be packed by skiers and snowmobiles. An unlimited amount of skiing terrain is located around the ranch; miles and miles of summer horse trails are wonderful for nordic skiing, while the bordering National Forest offers jeep trails and logging roads for backcountry skiing. The hay fields surrounding the ranch can be skied by beginners.

ACCOMMODATIONS

The Waunita Hot Springs Ranch has the capacity to hold about 80 people. The main lodge, where a variety of activities take place, contains the dining room, lobby, and the TV and library area. Guest rooms are carpeted and have private baths. Some rooms connect to provide suites for families. The Hillside Lodge contains several double rooms with private baths.

Three meals each day include buffet-style ranch cooking and are served in the large, sunny dining room. Fresh fruit and hot drinks are always available. No alcoholic beverages are allowed at the ranch.

The barn's top floor is a recreation room and music hall. Ping-pong tables, air hockey and game machines are available for those interested. The Pringles are musically inclined (they produced their own album in 1982) and will sometimes perform. The pool, with heated dressing rooms, is opened year round. An ice-skating rink will be added by 1986.

For a room and three meals, the regular rate is $40 per person; groups of 20 to 30 pay $37; groups of 31 to 45 pay $35; groups of 46 to 60 pay $33.50; and groups of more than 61 people pay $32. Without lunches the regular rate is $33; groups of 20 to 30 pay $30; groups of 31 to 60 pay $29; and groups of more than 61 people pay $27. All prices are per-person per-night, and include lodging and use of the trails, pool, game room and all ranch facilities.

RENTALS, INSTRUCTION AND GUIDED TOURS

No rentals are provided, though the Pringles will make arrangements in nearby Gunnison to have skis at the ranch for you upon arrival. The Pringles' son, Wes, can guide tours on the backcountry trails and is working on becoming a PSIA-certified instructor.

ACCESS

Waunita Hot Springs is located eight miles north of U.S. 50 between Monarch Pass and Gunnison. The turn-off to the ranch is marked by a sign a half mile west of Doyleville at the 176-mile marker. Gunnison is served by American and Trans-Colorado Airlines and Continental Trailways buses. The Pringles will meet skiers in Gunnison.

Contact Rod and Junelle Pringle, Waunita Hot Springs Ranch, 8007 County Road 887, Dept. 5M, Gunnison, Co. 81230, (303) 641-1266.

Conquistador Ski Area

Conquistador Ski Area, a downhill ski resort located in the San Isabel and Rio Grande National Forests, provides cross-country rentals and access to backcountry trails for touring in the Sangre De Christo Mountains. The cross-country ski shop, located in the alpine ski shop, rents 30 pairs of touring and telemark skis at $7 a set for a full day.

A map is provided by the resort to help you locate the trails, two of which are most frequently used. The Rainbow Trail is reached by the Conquistador ski lift for $2.50 for a one-lift lift ticket. A National Forest hiking and skiing trail that extends 100 miles from Salida to the Great Sand Dunes National Monument, the Rainbow Trail, for intermediate skiers, follows the 9,500 ft. contour. The Hermit Lake Trail, another intermediate National Forest trail, is seven miles or 11 km long and is located three miles by car from the ski area or can be reached by taking the Conquistador lift and skiing the first half mile of the Rainbow Trail. The $2.50 lift ticket applies here also.

Two instructors, one PSIA-certified, are available to teach lessons to skiers of all abilities. Instruction and guided tours are available by appointment only, the cost depends on the arrangements made.

Access from Pueblo: take Colorado 96 for 55 miles to Westcliffe. Conquistador Ski Area is located five miles west of Westcliffe on Colorado 96. A STOLport is located in Westcliffe, as are restaurants and motels for those planning overnight stays. For rental information, call (303) 783-9206.

Contact Art Hutchinson, Conquistador Ski Area, P.O. Box 347, Westcliffe, Co. 81252, (303) 783-9206.

Backcountry Trails

Salida area: Old Railroad Grade (E); Evans-Rush (E); South Cottonwood (EM); Iron City-Alpine (EM); Romley-Hancock (EM); Old Monarch Pass (EM); South Fooses Creek (MD); North Cottonwood.

The Salida Ranger District—San Isabel NF, 230 W. 16th St., Salida, 81201, 539-3591—administers the above.

Gunnison area: Old Monarch Pass (EM); Waunita Hot Springs (D).
Taylor Park area: Stagestop Meadows (EM); Union Park (EM); Red Creek Road (EM); Rainbow Lake Road (EM).
Ohio Creek area: Mill Creek (M).
Crested Butte area: Swampy Pass Trail (EM); Kebler Pass (EM); Mill Creek (EMD); Washington Gulch (EMD); Brush Creek-Pearl Pass (EMD); Gothic

Road (M); Splains Gulch (M); Cement Creek (M); Lake Irwin (MD); Walrod Gulch (D); Lily Lake-Floresta (D).

The Taylor River and Cebolla Ranger Districts—Gunnison NF, 216 N. Colorado, Gunnison, 81230, 641-0471—administer the above.

Paonia area: Clear Fork (E); Stevens Gulch (EM); Dark Canyon (EM); Kebler Pass (EM); Snowshoe Creek (EM); Hubbard Creek (MD).

Black Mesa area: Crystal Creek (EM); Curecanti Creek (EM).

The Paonia Ranger District—Gunnison NF, N. Rio Grande St., Paonia, 81428, 527-4131—administers the above.

Top of Grand Mesa: Scales Lakes (E); County Line (EM); Skyway Trail (EM); Connector Trail (EM); Crag Crest Loops (EMD).

The Grand Junction Ranger District—Grand Mesa-Uncompahgre NF, 4th and Rood, Grand Junction, 81501, 242-8211—administers the above.

West Grand Mesa: Old Grand Mesa Road (E); Mesa Lakes Trail (E); Long Slough (EM); Lake of the Woods (M); West Bench Trail (M); Anderson Reservoir No. 2 (MD); Lost Lake Trail (D).

The Collbran Ranger District—Grand Mesa NF, High St., Collbran, 81624, 487-3249—administers the above.

(E) Easier, (M) Moderate, (D) Difficult.

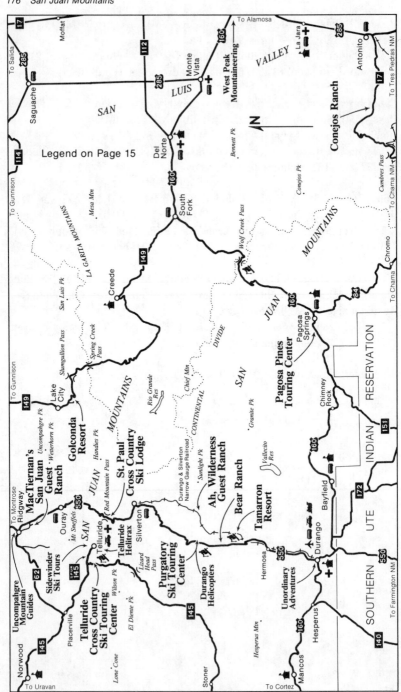

Legend on Page 15

San Juan Mountains

The San Juans contain several cross-country centers spread throughout this enormous mountain range. Starting in the north at Ridgway are Mac-Tiernan's San Juan Guest Ranch and the Uncompahgre Mountain Guides. Farther south, on the top of Red Mountain Pass is St. Paul Cross Country Ski Lodge. To the west of Ridgway and Red Mountain Pass is Telluride, the home of Telluride Cross Country Ski Touring Center, Telluride Helitrax and Sidewinder Ski Tours. South of Red Mountain Pass, and north of Durango, are Bear Ranch, Purgatory Ski Touring Center, Tamarron Resort, Durango Helicopters, Unordinary Adventures, and the Ah, Wilderness Guest Ranch, situated along the narrow-gauge railroad between Silverton and Durango. East of this area are Pagosa Pines Touring Center outside Pagosa Springs, Conejos Ranch in Antonito near the New Mexico border, and West Peak Mountaineering in La Veta.

This entire region, with the exception of La Veta, is in the San Juan Mountain Range. These mountains contain numerous 14,000 ft. peaks and are covered with snow for much of the year. Though avalanches can occur at any time and anywhere in the Rocky Mountains, the danger is extremely high in the San Juans. This has spawned the development of avalanche study and control and search-and-rescue operations.

Mining in the Telluride, Ouray and the Red Mountain Pass areas, together with ranching, has supported the San Juan region. Durango is the central point for several tourist attractions, including Mesa Verde National Park outside Cortez, and the Four Corners area; it is the starting point for the Durango-to-Silverton Narrow Gauge Railway. This train runs year round and snakes through El Canyon del Rio las Animas Perdidos, or the Canyon of the River of Lost Souls.

Downhill skiing can be enjoyed at Telluride and Purgatory ski areas, and Tamarron Resort. The cross-country ski industry has been growing since 1973, when the Bear Ranch became the first touring center in the area. Public cross-country trails are located at the Hillcrest Golf Course in Durango which has 1.6 miles of trails.

Durango and Montrose have their own airports, and Continental Trailways bus serves Durango, Ouray and Montrose. U.S. 550 connects Montrose and Durango and U.S. 160 is the major east-west highway.

Bear Ranch

Bear Ranch is owned and run by Ruedi and Leith Bear, former members of the Swiss and U.S. alpine ski teams. The Bears concern for environmental issues is reflected in the design of their ranch: all three modestly sized structures have solar panels and greenhouses, and blend well with the rural countryside.

Bear Ranch began in 1973 with the construction of its largest building, now a restaurant and ski rental shop. The ranch was originally a summer tennis club with what the Bears say are the only clay courts in Colorado. In 1981, two other buildings were added, giving the ranch the capacity to house 32 people in four condominiums. In the future, the Bears hope to build eight more condominiums and a central lodge.

In addition to cross-country skiing, activities in the area include alpine and nordic skiing at Purgatory ski area, sleigh rides, and ice fishing.

Bear Ranch is a member of the Colorado Cross Country Ski Association.

TRAILS

The trails at Bear Ranch are considered easier to moderate in comparison to those of other touring centers mentioned in this book.

Covering 530 acres, Bear Ranch is the oldest ski touring center in the southwest part of Colorado. There are close to 30 km of maintained trails: 5 km of beginner, 7 km of intermediate, and 15 km of advanced trails, all double-tracked. The trails wind around Haviland Lake and into some for-

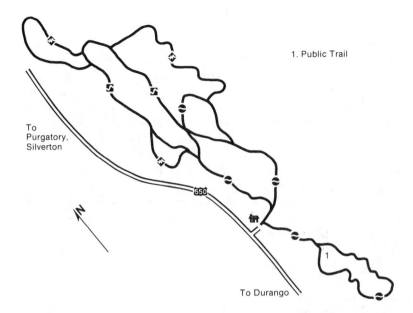

1. Public Trail

To
Purgatory,
Silverton

To Durango

ested areas. A nearby 5 km trail is maintained by the Bears and is free
to the public.

Trail access is free with equipment rental. The weekday trail fee is $1;
on weekends and holidays $2. Children under 12 may ski free; those from
age 12 to 18 pay $1. Trails are open to the public as well as to ranch guests.

ACCOMMODATIONS

Bear Ranch cannot be called a ranch in the western style...no animals
or crops are raised there. It is a sports ranch, featuring tennis in the summer and skiing in the winter.

Its four condominiums are set back from the highway and are connected
to one another by a room which holds a central hot tub. Each of the beau-
tifully designed condominiums can hold up to eight people, and is complete
with a fully equipped kitchen including a dishwasher and a coffee-maker,
a living room with television and cassette deck, a dining area, two bedrooms,
and two bathrooms, one with a jacuzzi tub. These are solar and wood heated
and are fully carpeted.

No meals are provided at the ranch, but dinner is served at the Bear
Ranch Restaurant adjacent to the condominiums. Grocery stores and convenience stores are located in Durango, 17 miles away.

Rates range from $100 to $175 per day per unit, depending on occupancy
and the season.

RENTALS AND INSTRUCTION

The ski rental equipment at Bear Ranch is replaced with new models every two years. The Bears carry 60 sets of Trak skis, mostly advanced, waxless touring skis. Guests at Bear Ranch may rent cross-country skis for $5 a day. For non-guests, adult and children's rentals for a half day are $7 and full-day rentals cost $10. The weekly rate is $36. A group of 15 or more people receives a discount of $1 per set. Gaiters can be rented for $1 a pair.

Ruedi, the only instructor, has had years of experience in both alpine and nordic skiing and can instruct all ability levels. Bear wrote his own book on downhill skiing techniques, "Pianta Su: Ski Like the Best," published by Little, Brown and Co. There is no telemarking at the ranch as the concentration is on track skiing.

During the busy season and the Christmas holidays, daily lessons are scheduled from 10 a.m. to 12 noon and 1 p.m. to 3 p.m. During the quieter seasons, lessons are given on Saturdays and Sundays only, at the above times. The cost is $15 per person for a two-hour lesson. The group rate for four is $10 per person.

RACES AND SPECIAL EVENTS

One event, called the Snowdown Citizen Race, has been held yearly since 1979 and includes 10 km, 7 km and 5 km races for anyone who wants to enter. Awards are given to the winners of classes based on age and sex.

ACCESS

Bear Ranch is located 17 miles north of Durango on Highway 550. Durango has air access to Denver and Albuquerque.

Contact Ruedi and Leith Bear, Bear Ranch, 42570 Highway 550, Dept. EE, Durango, Co. 81301, (303) 247-0111 or (303) 385-4764.

Golconda Resort

Golconda Resort differs from other touring centers in that no other Colorado resort offers helicopter skiing for nordic skiers together with a base lodge and excellent meals. Golconda, elevation 9,000 ft., is located outside Lake City on Lake San Cristobal. The largest natural lake in Colorado, it was formed 700 years ago when the Slumgullion slide, an enormous mud slide of volcanic ash, slid down to dam the Lake Fork River. You can see the slide from a vantage point above the resort.

Ron and Ella Jackson, the owners, have a Forest Service permit to fly to and use all of "Nordic Mountain" (they named it!) for cross-country downhill skiing. Covered with up to six feet of snow for most of the winter, Nordic Mountain stands at 12,500 ft. on the Continental Divide in the San Juan mountain range. From the top of the mountain, five 14,000 ft. peaks are visible. Skiers can be assured of safe, gentle, but exciting descents as the Forest Service, to avoid avalanche danger, does not allow heliskiing in the San Juans on slopes with more than a 23% grade.

The Jacksons plan to add alpine downhill skiing to their repertoire in 1986 and will separate the areas so telemarkers and alpine skiers will each have their own runs. The Jacksons want Golconda to become a heliskiing destination resort for all types of skiers.

THE TRIP

The helicopter departs from Golconda every day after skiers have received their helicopter and skiing briefing, and have been divided into groups of similar skiing abilities. Skis are lashed to the outside of the helicopter. Up to four passengers are allowed on each trip. After a five-minute ride from the resort to the top of the mountain, you are soon on your way.

Each group is led down the mountain by a guide. Fifty miles of terrain are used for ski runs, providing a variety of trips down the mountain. Two runs a day are made by each group and each run is different. All trips guarantee long slopes buried in powder with no uphill climbs—skiing is either on downhill slopes or level terrain. At the end of each run, the helicopter awaits to ferry skiers back to the summit or to the resort, a seven-minute trip as all ski runs head away from the lodge.

According to the Jacksons, Nordic Mountain provides 2,300 ft. of vertical fall—1,100 ft. in a beautiful alpine bowl and 1,200 ft. through timber to the base. Fall-line distance is 7-1/2 miles. Advanced beginners can average 2,200 vertical ft. and six to eight miles daily. Intermediate-or-better skiers can average 3,500 vertical ft. and 12 to 15 miles daily. An average of five hours of skiing can take place when conditions are right. Lunch is served on the mountain.

Trips up to Nordic Mountain are, of course, dependent on the weather; storms and high winds prevent the helicopter from flying. If this should happen, there are 10 miles of backcountry trails surrounding the resort that are available to skiers. (See map.) These trails are not groomed but they are marked.

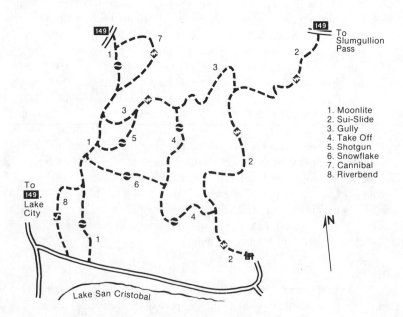

1. Moonlite
2. Sui-Slide
3. Gully
4. Take Off
5. Shotgun
6. Snowflake
7. Cannibal
8. Riverbend

RENTALS AND INSTRUCTION

Golconda carries 100 pairs of Fischer telemark skis and some Trak touring skis. For safety reasons, the Jacksons reserve the right to inspect all equipment brought into the resort...should your skis or bindings break while you are skiing in the deep snow on the mountain, your trip could be in jeopardy. Heavy mountaineering boots are available to rent.

Instruction is given by Ron and his son, Brett; both have been heliskiing for over nine years. The guide-to-skier ratio is kept at no more than one-to-eight.

It is recommended that skiers have at least one day of backcountry skiing experience before they attempt to heliski. The Jacksons feel skiers do not have to be advanced skiers to enjoy Nordic Mountain, and they encourage advanced beginners to try heliskiing with them. Being in good physical condition helps, especially when you are not used to the high altitudes of the San Juans. Techniques taught are not limited to one aspect of skiing; alpine, nordic and telemark methods are covered. Techniques can be practiced on the mountain.

Guiding and instruction are included in the various packages offered at the resort.

ACCOMMODATIONS

A variety of accommodations are available at Golconda, including motel rooms, cabins and apartments. The motel rooms are attached to the restaurant and lounge and hold up to four people. The apartments have one or two bedrooms and have fully equipped kitchens, sleeping room for six and an indoor picnic table for dining. The cabins include two bedrooms, fully equipped kitchens and fireplaces, and sleep up to six people.

The restaurant at Golconda is a wonderful surprise. For being so far from a large city, it has an enormous menu with daily specials. Choices are beef, fish and poultry, served with salads, potatoes and homemade ice cream. Many of the entrees are included in the American Plan, though a surcharge is added to the specialties. The menus are decorated with photographs of the ski trips taken from Golconda.

Several packages are offered and all include lodging, heliskiing with guides, three meals per day and taxes and tips. The bigger packages include a day of downhill skiing at Crested Butte, with transportation and lift ticket. Please inquire at Golconda as to what is offered in each package. Three days and two nights cost $207 per person, or $146 without meals. Four days and three nights cost $271 per person, or $183 without meals. Six days and five nights cost $549 per person, or $374 without meals. Eight days and seven nights cost $696 per person, or $538 without meals. A special group rate for two nights and one day costs $163 per person, or $130 without meals. Golconda has a group organizer plan in which a person can visit for no charge if he or she organizes a group of seven or more.

Included in the price are satellite TV, outdoor hot tub, ice skating and skate rentals.

ACCESS

Golconda is located about two miles south of Lake City. From Gunnison, take U.S. 50 five miles west to Colorado 149. Follow Colorado 149 for 47 miles to Lake City, and continue through the town until you reach a right turnoff to Lake San Cristobal. Take a left at the Golconda sign at the lake and follow for 1/4 mile.

Gunnison is served by American and Trans-Colorado Airlines and Continental Trailways buses. The Jacksons will shuttle skiers from Gunnison to the resort for $25 per person.

Contact Ron and Ella Jackson, Golconda Resort, P.O. Box 95, Lake City, Co. 81235, (303) 944-2256.

Pagosa Pines Touring Center

Pagosa Springs is a small town located on U.S. Highway 160 west of Wolf Creek Pass. Wolf Creek Pass is famous for the enormous amount of snow it receives—over 500 inches each year. Pagosa Pines Touring Center is situated west of Pagosa Springs at 7,300 ft., in the middle of a large planned community which includes condominiums, an athletic center, a hotel, a golf course, and a lake. The touring center and ski shop is located at the golf course clubhouse and has been in operation for four years. Dan Park, the manager at Pagosa since its beginning, has helped plan and implement the trail system.

TRAILS

The trails at Pagosa Pines Touring Center are rated easier in comparison to those of other touring centers mentioned in this book.

Fifteen kilometers of trails are maintained on the fairways of the golf course and around the neighboring homes over large open areas. The trails are 35% beginner, 55% intermediate and 10% advanced. These trails are excellent for training, practicing touring techniques and racing, as they have wide curves and long gentle downhill runs. Most of the trails are double-tracked.

Trail fees are $3.50 per day for the public. Property owners or lodge guests and members of the athletic clubs pay reduced rates. The touring center is open from 9 a.m. to 5 p.m. daily.

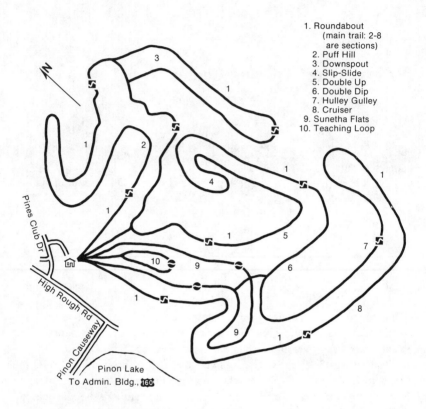

1. Roundabout
   (main trail: 2-8
   are sections)
2. Puff Hill
3. Downspout
4. Slip-Slide
5. Double Up
6. Double Dip
7. Hulley Gulley
8. Cruiser
9. Sunetha Flats
10. Teaching Loop

Pines Club Dr

High Rough Rd

Pinon Causeway

Pinon Lake
To Admin. Bldg., **160**

RENTALS AND INSTRUCTION

Eighty pairs of Trak skis are available to rent, including children's skis and track and mountaineering skis. The cost of renting for a full day is $8 for adults and $6 for children. After 1 p.m., the rental fee is $5. Skis, boots, and poles can be rented separately. Rentals for five days cost $32.

Three PSIA-certified instructors teach beginning through telemark lessons. The ski school is also certified by PSIA. Track skiing classes, beginning through advanced, are taught by appointment at 10:30 a.m. and 1:30 p.m. Telemarking is generally taught at a clinic, with evening classes at Pagosa Pines covering equipment and technique, and day classes at Wolf Creek ski area for on-the-slope instruction and practice.

A private track or telemark lesson costs $18 per hour. Semi-private lessons for two to three people are $12 per hour. Group lessons for four or more people are $8.50 per hour. The lift ticket at Wolf Creek is $16 for a full day and $11 for a half day for telemarkers.

GUIDED TOURS

A gourmet-lunch day tour can be arranged by appointment. This is a guided, instructional tour into the San Juan Mountains. The tour costs $18 per person for two to three people, or $14 per person for four or more people.

Day tours to various places in the area, including Williams Creek Lake for beginners and Wolf Creek Pass for advanced skiers, are available. Tours generally begin at 10 a.m. and run until 2 p.m. but can vary according to the overall ability of each group. Overnight snowcamping tours are also available. Arrangements for all these tours must be made in advance and the price depends on what sort of tour is arranged.

RACES AND SPECIAL EVENTS

Early in the season, clinics are given in preparation for a winter of skiing. In November, a ski care and preparation clinic is planned. In early December, both children's and adults' skiing clinics are held, snow permitting.

The Grizzly Chase Series, a series of three cross-country ski citizens' races, is held on the first Sunday of each month, January through March. The races include 5 km, 10 km and 20 km runs and prizes are awarded. This is a popular series and participation grows each year.

FOOD AND LODGING

There is a restaurant at the clubhouse which serves lunch during the winter months. Hot drinks are available most of the day.

The Sheraton Hotel at the Fairfield Pagosa Resort has many guest rooms, two restaurants and a lounge, as well as a health spa, meeting rooms and gift shop. The Sheraton offers a "Happy Trails Cross Country Ski Package," which includes room, trail fees, rentals, one gourmet day tour and tax, for $28 per person the first night and $18 per person each additional night; with a three-night minimum. Additional food and lodging is available in Pagosa Springs.

ACCESS

Pagosa Pines Touring Center is 55 miles east of Durango and three miles west of Pagosa Springs on U.S. 160. From Pagosa Springs, take a right turn into the Fairfield Pagosa complex and follow signs to the golf course clubhouse.

Contact Dan Park, Pagosa Pines Touring Center, P.O. Box 4040, Pagosa Springs, Co. 81157, (303) 731-4141, ext. 4155.

Purgatory Ski Touring Center

The Purgatory Ski Touring Center, located 25 miles north of Durango in the southern San Juan Mountains, has been operated by Purgatory ski resort since 1980. Under a five-year commitment to the center, the ski resort will continue to assist the center in upgrading maintenance equipment and enlarging the number of trails at the touring center.

Tony Forrest, the director of the touring center, has been with the center since 1982. Forrest is the director of the Demonstration Team for PSIA; the demo team is a group which meets in different parts of the country several times a year to demonstrate and teach new cross-country skiing techniques to instructors. He is also a guide for Durango Helicopters and discusses cross-country skiing in the Durango area on a local radio spot.

The touring center is the hub for the "Nords of Wolverton," a zany group of cross-country skiers known for their willingness to do anything involving snow and a couple of skis. Helicopter skiing and alpine skiing are also offered near the center.

Purgatory Ski Touring Center is a member of the Colorado Cross Country Ski Association.

TRAILS

The trails at Purgatory Ski Touring Center are moderate in comparison to those of other touring centers mentioned in this book.

The 15 km of groomed trails cross terrain that is approximately 25%beginner, 50% intermediate and 25% advanced. Trails are double-

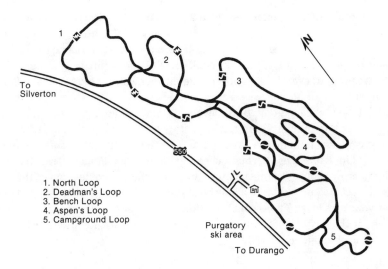

1. North Loop
2. Deadman's Loop
3. Bench Loop
4. Aspen's Loop
5. Campground Loop

tracked; additional tracks are set at the traffic areas near the touring center. The trails wind across meadows, around a reservoir and into forests; there are occasional scenic overlooks with views of the West Needle Mountains. There is no access from the trails to backcountry terrain, since the touring center is bordered on one side by U.S. 550 and on another by the West Needle Mountains. Severe avalanche danger is ever-present in the surrounding mountains.

Plans to expand the trail system for the winter of 1985-86 will add 5 more kilometers of trails, most likely for beginner and intermediate skiers.

The trail fees are $3 for one day, $5 for two days, $7 for three days and $9 for four days. The touring center is open seven days a week. Purgatory's alpine lift ticket may be exchanged for access to the trails and lessons at the touring center.

RENTALS AND INSTRUCTION

Purgatory Ski Touring Center has 50 pairs of Rossignol and Trak skis available for rent, including skis for children. The skis are all waxless touring skis. Rentals cost $10 for a full day and $6 for a half day.

This is a PSIA-certified ski school and three of the five instructors are fully certified. All levels of skiing are taught, including telemarking. Lessons are given at 1 p.m. seven days a week and on Saturday and Sunday at 10 a.m. Fees are $13 per person for a group lesson and $20 for both lesson and rentals. A family lesson for two members is $24, plus $6 for each additional member. Private lessons cost $25 for track or telemark lessons plus $6 for each additional person. All the above prices include the trail fee. Groups of 10 or more receive a 20% discount on lessons, rentals and trail fees.

Telemark lessons, given at Purgatory ski area, cost the same as the lessons mentioned above, plus an additional $10 for a lift ticket.

Among the several clinics offered are the following: every Sunday at 9:30 a.m. a free half-hour cross-country workshop is held for those who buy a trail ticket; once a month a free two-hour track clinic is given for all abilities with the purchase of a trail ticket; a free three-hour telemark clinic is given once a month to skiers of all abilities (a lift ticket must be purchased for $10). These telemark clinics are quite popular and attract a large number of people. Ten instructors are available to provide you with personal attention, and there are several group divisions so that you can ski at your own level. Those who have taken the clinic can use the lifts for the rest of the day. The touring center has plans to institute a telemark race after each clinic as of 1986.

GUIDED TOURS

In 1985, Forrest initiated several local tours including natural history tours, some with winter touring seminars; a Mesa Verde tour, at Mesa Verde National Park; and a winter photography tour. He hopes to create a natural history trail at the center in 1986. These local tours will continue in the future.

RACES AND SPECIAL EVENTS

Purgatory Ski Touring Center has a fairly heavy race schedule each year. The races are mostly local citizens' races and skiers can accumulate points at some of them for an award at the end of the season. The races range from 3 km to 30 km events and all have classes divided by age and sex.

A 5 km and 10 km race is held in early December; the Rossignol Demo Day, a 3x5 relay race, is run in mid-December; a 7.5 and 15 km race occurs in mid-January; the Durango Langlauf 5, 15 and 30 km race is held at the end of January; a 10 and 20 km race runs in early February; La Plata Community Hospital sponsors a 3x5 relay at the end of February; a 7.5, 15, and 30 km race is held in early March; and Wolverton Days, in mid-March, is Purgatory's festival race—a two-day fun-fest with costume races, food, Gelande ski jumps and plenty of fun.

A program for local school children, which includes a half day of skiing and lessons, is given five times each year. In addition to cross-country skiing, children can also learn about backcountry skiing and natural history through this program.

FOOD AND LODGING

Food and lodging are available at Purgatory ski area and at several locations along U.S. 550 between Purgatory and Durango. There are many restaurants and motels in Durango, 25 miles south of the touring center.

ACCESS

Purgatory Ski Touring Center is located across the highway from Purgatory ski area, on U.S. 550, 25 miles north of Durango. There is air access to Durango from Denver and Albuquerque.

Contact Tony Forrest, Purgatory Ski Touring Center, P.O. Box 666-EE, Durango, Co. 81301, (303) 247-9000 ext. 3196.

Tamarron Resort

Tamarron, located north of Durango, is a year-round resort with a variety of accommodations from lodge rooms to executive condominiums. Tamarron's winter facilities include cross-country ski trails, indoor tennis, indoor and outdoor swimming, an alpine ski training area complete with a lift, and ice skating.

Tamarron has been offering cross-country skiing since its beginning in 1975 and in 1980 began maintaining trails. Buses leave every 15 minutes from Tamarron and take guests to and from nearby Purgatory ski area.

TRAILS
The trails at Tamarron are rated easier in comparison to those of other touring centers mentioned in this book.

Seven kilometers of trails, including beginner and intermediate trails, are maintained. Set on the golf course, they are gently rolling meadow-like trails. No advanced terrain is available. The trails are double-tracked and are constantly groomed because of frequent visits from local elk. Because Tamarron is located on U.S. 550, no access to backcountry trails is available. A nearby area called Rockwood (an old historic town) can be reached from the trails and is sometimes skied by guests.

Guests may ski the trails free of charge. Marked by blue diamonds showing direction, all trails lead from the tennis clubhouse at the bottom of the

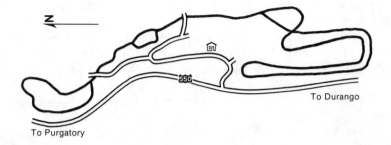

hill below the lodge. Restrooms and soda machines are located at the clubhouse.

The alpine ski hill can be used for telemarking.

ACCOMMODATIONS

There are three restaurants located at the resort. These are Le Canyon, which provides a gourmet menu, The San Juan Room, a more casual restaurant with traditional family meals, and The Caboose, an old-fashioned ice cream parlor that serves sandwiches and snacks.

Guests can either stay in rooms at the main lodge or rent fully equipped condominiums. Rates for accommodations range from $66 a night for a single room to over $200 a night for townhouses. Rates vary according to the type of room, occupancy, and the season, and special packages are available. Inquire for more specific rates.

Also available for guests is a Spa/Health Club which includes a pool, a hot tub, steam and sauna facilities, a fitness room where athletic programs are held, and a full array of therapeutic massages from massage therapists.

Child care facilities are plentiful—there is a staff babysitter for the evenings and a day program for children four to 10 years old. Activities include snow games, arts and crafts, swimming, water games, tennis, ping pong, and ski lessons. Child care for a half day costs $10; a full day is $18, lunch included. Children can learn to downhill or cross-country ski.

Beauty and barbershops, movies, heliskiing, and broomball are also available.

RENTALS AND INSTRUCTION

Purgatory ski resort has a ski rental and retail shop, which includes cross-country skis, in Tamarron's lodge. By 1986, they hope to have some telemarking equipment available for rent.

Lessons are given by two full-time instructors, both with many years of skiing and instructing experience. Although all levels of skiing can be taught, because of the absence of advanced terrain mostly beginner and intermediate lessons are given.

Group lessons are available for $12 per person. Lessons are given every day at 10 a.m. and at 1 p.m. Skiers are asked to register by 6 p.m. the day prior to the lesson. Private instruction is available for $25 per person plus $10 for each additional person. A maximum of two people is allowed for private lessons. Registration is required by 6 p.m. the evening before the lesson.

Telemark lessons are given at the alpine hill. One hour of private telemark instruction costs $20 per lesson. Twenty-four hours' advance notice is requested.

GUIDED TOURS

Skiers are generally guided around the trails or down to Rockwood. Daily tours are given from 12 noon to 3 p.m. and cost $18 per person. A minimum of two people and twenty-four hours' advance notice is required. Lunches are available.

Wine and cheese tours and moonlight tours can be arranged and prices vary according to the tour planned.

ACCESS

Tamarron is located 18 miles north of Durango on U.S. 550. There is an airport in Durango with flights from Denver and Albuquerque.

Contact Kathy Eppich, Tamarron Resort, P.O. Box 3131-EE, Durango, Co. 81301, (303) 247-8801. For reservations, call (800) 525-5420 nationwide; (800) 525-0493 in Colorado.

Telluride Cross Country Ski Touring Center

Telluride Nordic Center has some of the most fantastic vistas of any ski area in Colorado. The trails begin at 9,000 ft., where there are unobstructed panoramas of the San Juan mountain range, including some 14,000 ft. peaks. The Nordic Center has been run in some capacity since the Telluride Ski Resort opened in 1972 and has been operating out of the present cabin, an old homestead, for three years.

TRAILS

The trails at Telluride Nordic Center are rated moderate in comparison to those of other touring centers mentioned in this book.

Twenty-two kilometers of trails are groomed, maintained and double-tracked. The majority of trails are intermediate and advanced, though the easier trails are long enough for a beginner to spend a good amount of time skiing. The trails wind through forests of pine and aspen and travel over meadows.

Backcountry skiing is accessible from the trails. Boomerang Road, accessible from Jerry's Hill or Cabin's Ridge trails, takes skiers to Prospect Basin and affords some very nice intermediate to advanced backcountry skiing.

The track fee is $4 a day. The trails are open from 9 a.m. to 4:30 p.m. daily. One day of the Telluride ski area multi-day ski pass is exchangeable for a day of lessons and skiing at the nordic center.

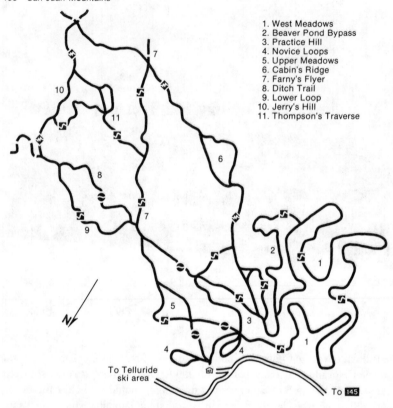

1. West Meadows
2. Beaver Pond Bypass
3. Practice Hill
4. Novice Loops
5. Upper Meadows
6. Cabin's Ridge
7. Farny's Flyer
8. Ditch Trail
9. Lower Loop
10. Jerry's Hill
11. Thompson's Traverse

To Telluride
ski area

To **145**

RENTALS AND INSTRUCTION

Thirty pairs of Fischer waxless touring skis are available to rent. If telemarking skis are desired, skiers are sent to rental outlets in Telluride. A full-day rental of skis, boots and poles is $8 and afternoon half-day rentals are $6.

All levels of track skiing are taught by as many as nine full- and part-time instructors, all PSIA-certified; the ski school is also certified with PSIA. Two-hour group lessons are given daily at 10:50 a.m. and at 1:50 p.m. Lessons cost $17 for adults and $14 for children under 12.

Track and technique orientation lessons are given every day by prior arrangement for the intermediate-or-better skier. The lessons feature guided tours of the trails and pointers on technique. The cost is $11 per hour.

Telemark lessons are held on Tuesdays at 10:50 a.m. and 1:50 p.m. at Telluride ski area. Skiers are met at the Meadows Base and lift tickets are required. The cost is $17 plus lift ticket for two hours of instruction. Private lessons are given by arrangement and cost $30 per hour, plus $15 for each additional person.

The Nordic Package, three- or five-day ski packages, includes skiing and lessons. Day one of the three-day package starts with an intensive two-hour lesson with a video analysis and track skiing. Day two includes a two-hour track and technique orientation or telemark lesson and track skiing. The third day includes a half-day backcountry tour with lunch. The total cost, not including a lift ticket for telemarking, is $75, or $95 with equipment rentals. The first day of the five-day package is the same as the first day above. The second day, the track and technique orientation lesson is given along with track skiing. On the third day, a two-hour telemark lesson is held. On days four and five the skier can choose either a full-day tour and a day of skiing on the track, or a half-day backcountry tour, each day exploring different areas. The cost is $125, or $160 with rentals.

Five track-skiing clinics are given every year. These clinics are scheduled on Saturdays and the techniques taught depend on each group's interest at the time.

GUIDED TOURS

Guides lead backcountry tours to several areas in the San Juan Mountains, all on National Forest land. Some of the places visited are Wilson Mesa, Lizard Head Pass, and Prospect Basin. These tours must be arranged in advance and are tailored to the abilities of the participants. The cost for a half-day tour is $35 for the first person plus $15 for each additional person. The full-day tour is $50 for the first person plus $20 for each additional person. Both tours include lunch.

RACES AND SPECIAL EVENTS

Several races are sponsored each year. Telluride Nordic Center holds a series of four Nordic Cup races, each one different but including relay races and 5 km, 10 km and 30 km events. Four Telemark races, three of which are Grand Slalom races, are held each year. Five more races defy single classification and range from the Nordic "Up and Down," which includes an upslope and downslope race, the Annual Butch Cassidy 10 km race, the Summit Series Telemark Race, the Annual Telluride Classic X-C Race (15, 30, and 50 km, including a barbeque) and the April Fool's San Juan Quad-A-Thon, which includes downhill skiing, cross-country skiing, running and biking by one person or a team. All races have their own individual entry fees and award schedules.

FOOD AND LODGING

Telluride, a Victorian mining town, is located less than five miles from the Telluride Nordic Center and has a variety of accommodations and restaurants. Telluride's central reservations number is 1-800-525-3455. In

Colorado, 728-4431. Or write Telluride Central Reservations, P.O. Box 1009, Telluride, Co. 81435.

ACCESS

From Montrose and Grand Junction, drive to Ridgway via U.S. 550. Turn right on Colorado 62 to Colorado 145 and turn left toward Telluride. At the junction of the Colorado 145 Spur into Telluride, continue right on Colorado 145 for one mile, and turn left onto the ski area road; continue for a half mile to the nordic center on the right.

Contact Jim Pettegrew, Telluride Nordic Center, P.O. Box 307, Telluride, Co. 81435 (303) 728-3404 ext. 3856.

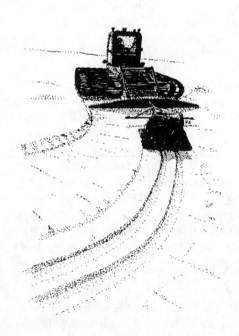

Ah, Wilderness Guest Ranch

Ah, Wilderness Guest Ranch, at 7,473 ft., is located in El Canyon del Rio las Animas Perdidos (The Canyon of the River of Lost Souls). The historic narrow-gauge railroad that snakes through the canyon on its way from Durango to Silverton (but just to Cascade Canyon in the winter) provides the only transportation to the ranch. Ah, Wilderness is surrounded by the San Juan National Forest and is bordered by the Weminuche Wilderness Area.

Guests may stay in one of several rustic cabins, which can accommodate four to 10 people each and are furnished with woodstoves and full baths. Home-cooked meals are served family-style in the main lodge.

The trails cater to the novice skier. In the past, 5 km of trails were maintained, though Larry Hays, the owner, plans to offer up to 10 km of packed trails by the 1985-86 season. Trails follow the river and enter the National Forest; these are also used as horse trails in the summer. No other backcountry skiing is accessible from the ranch because of the canyon's narrow size.

Fifteen pairs of waxless touring skis are available to guests at no charge. In addition to skiing, you can enjoy sleigh rides, snowshoeing, ice skating, and a hot tub. Helicopter skiing is offered through Durango Helicopters. No instruction is provided at Ah, Wilderness Guest Ranch.

Weekly rates are $450 per adult and include lodging, meals, and the use of all ranch facilities. Daily rates are $90 for adults, a 20% discount for children ages two to 12, and children under two are free. The winter season runs from early December to mid-January.

Access from Durango: take the Durango & Silverton Narrow Gauge Railway 23 miles to the ranch (the ranch is midway between the towns).

Contact Larry Hays, Ah, Wilderness Guest Ranch, P.O. Box 997, Durango, Co. 81302, (303) 247-4121.

Conejos Ranch

Conejos Ranch is located in the Conejos River Canyon, 15 miles south-west of Antonito, close to the New Mexico border. Originally a 19th century hunting lodge, and purchased in 1980 by Bill and Wendy Haberlin, it is a 92-acre ranch surrounded by the Rio Grande National Forest. Cross-country skiing is available on maintained trails and a two-acre lake provides the setting for ice skating.

Conejos Ranch is a member of the Colorado Cross Country Ski Association.

Guests can stay in either the lodge or in six outlying cabins complete with fully equipped kitchens. Visitors have the choice of eating at the ranch restaurant, which serves traditional ranch fare for breakfast, lunch and dinner, or cooking their own meals.

The Haberlins maintain five kilometers of cross-country trails on their ranch. Their ski shop offers 75 pairs of LMS and Norsemark touring skis, both waxable and waxless, for rent. They also rent snowshoes and ice skates. One cross-country ski race is held near the Ides of March in mid-March. Full-moon ski bashes and pot-luck dinners end with a dip in the hot tub. Telemarking and backcountry skiing are both available. Telemark and racing clinics are held during the season.

The rates at Conejos are: $54 per day for two people for a cabin; lodge rooms cost $25 per night for a single and $35 for a double. Additional guests in cabins or rooms, including children, cost $9 each. Prices include the use of the game room, video movies, and the hot tub.

Access from Alamosa: take U.S. 285 to Antonito. Pick up Colorado 17 southwest and follow for 15 miles to Conejos Ranch.

Contact Bill and Wendy Haberlin, Conejos Ranch, Antonito, Co. 81120, (303) 376-5623.

MacTiernan's San Juan Guest Ranch

The San Juan Guest Ranch is run by Scott MacTiernan and his mother, Pat. The ranch is located in a beautiful valley below the San Juan Mountains outside Ridgway. It is in such a scenic location that many commercials and advertisements depicting rugged ranchers or outdoor enthusiasts have been filmed and photographed here. The MacTiernans describe their ranch as a "secret place of unforgettable beauty." The ranch has been run as a family-style guest ranch for seven years. Lately, during the winter, it has been open for prearranged groups only.

The San Juan Guest Ranch is a member of the Colorado Cross Country Ski Association.

TRAILS

The trails at the San Juan Guest Ranch are rated moderate in comparison to those of other touring centers mentioned in this book.

Miles upon miles of backcountry skiing terrain lie adjacent to the ranch. MacTiernan transports his guests via snowmobile to the top of Miller Mesa, where logging roads offer beginning to intermediate ski terrain. Advanced runs can be made on the descent from the top of the mesa.

MacTiernan maintains many easier trails on the ranch, all of which are packed by snowmobile. The estimated combined mileage of the trails, including the logging roads and the trails maintained on the ranch, is close to 50 miles.

ACCOMMODATIONS

The ranch is centered around a lodge which contains a dining room and a large living area decorated with the photographs used in the commercials filmed at the ranch. The lodge is solar-heated and fully carpeted. Guests stay in a collection of apartments, each capable of holding from four to eight people. The apartments are comfortably furnished, some with bedroom lofts; all are complete with kitchen facilities and private baths. The average number of guests at the ranch is 15; the maximum capacity is 20. This small number helps promote a personal touch to everyone's stay.

Other winter pastimes offered at the ranch include a jacuzzi, sleigh rides, snow-tubing and snowshoeing.

The San Juan Guest Ranch is a year-round facility that offers horseback riding and fishing in the summer and hunting in the fall. Photography workshops are offered in the fall. The ranch is filled with affectionate animals, from cats to horses, most of them looking for attention.

The ranch has a reputation for its attention to meals. Trained chefs are hired to provide gourmet-style cuisine for all the meals served. Three meals are served daily to guests; the price is included in the nightly rates.

In addition to meals, rates include lodging, maid service, use of skiing trails and all other activities. The prices range from $50 a day for children under five to $120 a day for adults, single occupancy. Weekly rates range from $200 a week for children under five to $600 per week for adults, single occupancy. Reservations are necessary.

RENTALS AND INSTRUCTION

MacTiernan, the only instructor at the ranch, is a PSIA-certified instructor and has taught four years of downhill skiing at Aspen. He is capable of teaching all levels of skiing, from beginner to telemark. The beginning lessons are given on the easier trails right on the ranch; more advanced lessons are given on the trails adjacent to the ranch.

No ski rentals are available at the ranch. If equipment is needed, MacTiernan can assist in arranging for ski rentals from a local store.

ACCESS

Follow U.S. 550 to approximately four miles south of Ridgway to the Potter Ranch sign and the intersection of Colorado 23. Turn south onto Colorado 23. Cross the river bridge and take an immediate left. The stone entrance to San Juan Ranch is one mile from the bridge on the left. MacTiernan provides free shuttle service to and from the airport in Montrose.

Contact Scott MacTiernan, MacTiernan's San Juan Guest Ranch, 2882 Colorado 23, Ridgway, Co. 81432, (303) 626-5360.

St. Paul Cross Country Ski Lodge

The St. Paul Lodge is located at the top of Red Mountain Pass, on a twisty, curvy, and, in the winter, very avalanche-prone highway through the San Juan Mountains. The lodge overlooks a dramatic 180-degree panorama of the San Juans above timberline. Sitting at 11,440 ft., the lodge is the highest of any described in this book.

The lodge's unique feature is that you must ski one mile in from the highway with your belongings. You are advised to pack lightly in a backpack or duffel bag to make the transport of your luggage easier. Potential visitors are given a list of appropriate clothing to pack. Because of the elevation and the demands of the skiing in this area, visitors are expected to be in good physical condition and to have had a doctor's checkup before arrival if there are any health problems.

TRAILS

The skiing at St. Paul Cross Country Ski Lodge is rated more difficult in comparison to skiing at other touring centers mentioned in this book.

When skiers arrive, they are met at the highway with rental equipment and are guided and instructed, if necessary, for the one-mile trek to the lodge.

There is no set track at St. Paul, though the trail to the lodge is packed by snowmobile. The skiing in the area is on difficult terrain and Chris George, the owner, helps his guests learn the cross-country downhill techniques necessary to ski it. He insists on guiding guests because of the severe avalanche danger everywhere. Since the safe areas to ski are not far from the dangerous areas, use of a guide is imperative.

This lodge is not part of a hut system; it is isolated and there is no point-to-point skiing in the area. All skiing begins and ends at the lodge.

ACCOMMODATIONS

George built his rustic lodge in 1973 over the mine shaft of the old St. Paul mine. The lodge was once a "tipple house," which gets its name from the way the ore was taken from the mine: it was lifted out of the shaft in large buckets, and the buckets were tipped to pour the ore into the cars of the train transporting it. The lodge was built from lumber from old nearby structures, wood from a torn-down church in Denver and rough-cut lumber.

The lodge's capacity is 22 people at one time. There are two dormitory rooms and four private rooms: all share two washrooms and showers and a toilet. There is no electricity at the lodge, but there is hot water and a sauna.

The cooking is supervised by George, who is British, and who served a full apprenticeship as a chef in England. Food is served family-style in a small dining room on the lower level of the lodge. The lounge and sleeping quarters are upstairs on the second floor.

The charge, $55 to $65 a day, includes dorm space or private rooms, three meals a day, ski rentals, instruction and guiding. Group rates are available.

RENTALS AND INSTRUCTION

George outfits all his guests with his 22 pairs of skis and boots. He has mountaineering skis with metal edges, and all the bindings are A.B.C. Joffa-type cable bindings, which will not tear up boots during downhill runs. His boots are old, heavy, downhill boots.

George and one other resident guide do all of the instructing. George taught at Colorado Outward Bound for 10 years, was a British Mountaineering Association Guide/Instructor, and has 22 years of experience in international climbing and skiing. He has also been the site director of three international speed skiing championships in Silverton. He teaches mainly cross-country downhill techniques, including but not restricted to telemarking. He feels that beginners on cross-country skis have no trouble learning these techniques and that he sends his guests away with strengths and new skills instead of merely having entertained them.

Since all lessons are geared to the needs and desires of the group, it is up to the individuals to decide among themselves whether they would like to have an all-day clinic or would prefer to learn while skiing.

Two other local instructors in Silverton are on call for those days when more instructors are needed.

GUIDED TOURS

As mentioned before, all trips out of the lodge are guided. The avalanche danger is so severe in some places, George will not risk letting his guests roam by themselves. But there are many safe areas to ski. Moonlight tours are given when the moon and weather cooperate. Expert powder tours, with a shuttle back to the lodge, are offered.

In the spring, George can lead tours on a "haute route" (high route) trail from Silverton to Telluride and Ouray. There are no huts in this area, so skiers must set up tents or stay in small mountain towns enroute.

ACCESS

From Ouray or Montrose, take U.S. 550 to about 150 yards south of the Red Mountain Pass summit, where there is a plowed parking space. A packed trail leads from there to the lodge. The St. Paul offers pick-up service from Montrose Airport for a $15 charge. Continental Trailways bus can stop at the top of Red Mountain Pass.

Contact Chris George, The St. Paul Cross Country Ski Lodge, P.O. Box 463, Silverton, Co. 81433, (303) 387-5494, or 387-5367.

Uncompahgre Mountain Guides

Uncompahgre Mountain Guides is run by James and Diane Burwick. Their philosophy of maintaining good communications with their clients begins when the skier first inquires about his or her trip. The guides need to find out what the skier's capabilities are, but most of all, what the skier wants to accomplish and experience on his or her ski vacation. Once that is known, the logistics and the planning are up to the guides. Each tour is structured according to the desires of the group and are ideal for those with a limited amount of time for vacationing. The skier just has to arrive in Ridgway and he or she will be taken care of.

All tours take place in the San Juan Mountains and can range from one-day tours in the Last Dollar and Dallas Divide areas, to four-day and three-night 25-mile tours along the Dallas Trail. Tours from town to town, Ouray to Lake City, Ouray to Telluride, or Ouray to Silverton can be arranged, and there are guided day tours up Red Mountain Pass. Prices vary according to the tour chosen and how many days are spent skiing.

The Dallas Trail is an old and once well-used cattle trail that connects Ouray and Telluride. The trail is 25 miles long and skirts the Mt. Sneffels range. The Burwicks have been working with the Forest Service to get permission to set up a tepee along the trail to be used for overnight shelter, but a permanent location for the tepee has not been decided on. Tents are used in the meantime. The Dallas Trail is very difficult to follow and the country is quite rugged, but there is almost no avalanche danger along the trail. There are three alternate routes for those who do not want to ski the entire length of the trail. The price for a week with the guides, including two days' acclimation and a three-night, four-day trip is $550 for one person and $925 for two.

The Burwicks pamper their clients. If time allows, they prefer to spend a day or so helping clients recuperate from jet lag and getting to know each skier's capabilities. They give ski lessons, discuss problems occasionally encountered at high altitudes, and instruct in the use of avalanche beacons. Then the tour can begin, or a day can be spent skiing and practicing.

The Burwicks stress that the use of a guide can actually maximize the clients' vacation time—each day can be enjoyed without the bother of planning where to eat and sleep or what to do the next day. The guide's job is one of service: to help the skier learn and experience as much as possible during his limited vacation time. The skier-to-guide ratio is kept very low, usually two skiers to one guide. Groups of no more than four people are taken on each tour.

Package trips are available. These include a five-day bed-and-breakfast tour of the San Juans, or a five-day winter-orientation tour, to name two.

The Uncompahgre Mountain Guides also guide trips overseas, usually to South America. They can guide ice- and rock-climbing tours, backpacking trips and more. Inquire with them for more information.

Contact James and Diane Burwick, Uncompahgre Mountain Guides, P.O. Box 313-B, Ridgway, Co. 81432, (303) 626-5776.

Unordinary Adventures

Unordinary Adventures was set up in 1985 by a group of three men—Arnie Eversull, Bill Leo and Ron Schermacher—as a guide referral service and booking agent business in which skiers and outdoorspersons looking for specific adventures were paired with the guide services that could assist them. Responding to a need for "hut skiing" in the San Juan region, the group has since developed a ski touring program that includes the use of a tepee.

The trail to the tepee, originating at Purgatory ski area, is a beginner-level trail and can be skied with or without guides. To reach the tepee, you must ski along the Cascade Divide Road for 15 km; it is located below Gray Rock Peak in the San Juan National Forest. Avalanche danger on the trail and around the tepee is low, though areas prone to avalanches exist within skiing distance. The terrain surrounding the tepee varies from open, rolling hills to steep chutes for additional skiing.

The tepee is stocked with stove and fuel, sleeping mats, lanterns, cooking and eating utensils, water, and certain basic food supplies. Skiers are responsible for providing their own equipment, clothes and food.

Tours, usually two or more days in length, can be taken from the beginning of December to the end of May, snow permitting. There are two full-time and four part-time guides at Unordinary Adventures; all are experienced skiers, teach nordic skiing, have advanced first-aid and CPR training, and are knowledgeable in backcountry rescue. When groups are guided, Unordinary Adventures provides all safety equipment and food. Guided tours cost $60 per person per day; hut rental is $10 per person per night. Group discounts are available. Personal equipment lists and trip information are available on request. Groups without guides must pick up a key for locked camp boxes (where supplies are stored) from Gold Medal Sports in Durango.

Access: Purgatory Ski Area is located on U.S. 550, 25 miles north of Durango.

Contact Ron Schermacher, Unordinary Adventures, P.O. Box 1415-CCCS, Durango, Co. 81302, (303) 247-1541.

West Peak Mountaineering

West Peak Mountaineering offers guide service to the 100 miles of touring trails in the San Isabel National Forest surrounding the town of La
Veta. None of these trails are maintained and they are suited to all levels
of skiers. Elevations range from 7,000 ft. to 13,000 ft. in areas from the
Old La Veta Pass west of La Veta to Cordova Pass near the Spanish Peaks.
All the trails in this area are unmarked, and unless you are acquainted with
them, they can be confusing; guides familiar with these backcountry trails
are advised. The ski season in the Spanish Peaks area lasts from Thanksgiving to Easter.

Four guides, some of whom are certified by PSIA, have from five to 20
years of skiing and teaching experience and are familiar with the local flora
and fauna as well as the trails. Most tours given are day tours and cost
$17 a day for a certified guide, or $7 a day for a non-certified guide. Overnight ski and winter camping trips can be arranged. On these trips, skiers
stay in tents and carry their own food. The charge for a guide for an overnight tour depends on the size of the group, the length and the destination
of the tour. Some other trips offered are moonlight tours, wine-and-cheese
tours and photography tours.

West Peak Mountaineering rents touring equipment from their retail shop
in La Veta; Trak and Fischer waxless touring skis and some waxable skis
are available. Children can be outfitted. Rentals are $6 for a full day, $4.50
for a half day, $11 for two days, and $16 for three days. This is also the
location of a mountaineering shop with a full line of equipment for the summer and winter outdoor enthusiast.

West Peak Mountaineering and the 1899 Bed and Breakfast Inn in La
Veta offer a Cross Country Ski Package which includes lodging, rental
equipment, breakfast and a packed lunch, guide service and basic cross-
country instruction at a discounted rate. Rates vary according to the size
of the group.

La Veta is located 16 miles southwest of Walsenburg. Take U.S. 160 west
from Walsenburg for 13 miles to Colorado 12, follow Colorado 12 south
to La Veta.

Contact Carmen Goodwin, West Peak Mountaineering, P.O. Box 459,
La Veta, Co. 81055, (303) 742-3661.

Durango Helicopters

Durango Helicopters has a permit with the United States Forest Service covering 500 square miles of the San Juan National Forest near Durango
and Silverton. Tours begin in late November and continue well into May.

Skiing runs are chosen for intermediate and expert skiers, with elevations as high as 13,000 ft. and vertical descents of 1,000 to 3,800 ft.

As avalanches are always a potential danger in these mountains, rescue transceivers are distributed, informal safety seminars are given before each tour, and guides are trained in avalanche awareness and proper route selection.

Ski groups meet every day and leave from the Purgatory Ski Touring Center. Prices are $45 for one intermediate-to-expert run of 1,500 vertical feet; a half day of three intermediate-to-expert runs, with a minimum of 5,000 ft. and a maximum of 8,000 vertical feet, costs $145; a full day of seven advanced-to-expert runs, a minimum of 10,000 ft. and a maximum of 16,000 vertical feet, costs $255. Additional skiing is $30 per run and requires agreement by the entire skiing group.

Packages are offered and include heliskiing, lodging at nearby Tamarron Resort and meals, and range from $792 to $1,460 depending on length of stay and activities planned.

Contact Durango Helicopters, P.O. Box 1637, Durango, Co. 81301, (303) 247-9620.

Sidewinder Ski Tours

Sidewinder Ski Tours operates under an outfitter-guide permit from the United States Forest Service in the San Juan Mountains and in Arches National Park and the La Sal Mountains of southeastern Utah. Tours range from one-day ski tours to week-long heli-ski vacations and are available from mid-December to mid-May. Skiing is done in groups of four to eight skiers to one guide. At the staging area before take-off, skiers are given a safety and logistics orientation and are then grouped according to skiing ability.

Both nordic and alpine downhill skiers can be accommodated; high-alpine tours can be designed to meet special needs of each group. Skiers should be of strong and advanced abilities and be familiar with deep snow conditions; they must have the ability to control their speed and maintain stability in a multitude of soft snow conditions. Instruction is given on an informal basis as needed.

Sidewinder Ski Tours offers three different tours, averaging from 2,000 to 3,000 vertical feet. The one-day package provides five runs at $205 a day. Additional skiing costs $30 per run. The weekend tour and one-week tour combine heli-skiing and alpine skiing at the Telluride ski resort, with lodging and meals at the rustic Skyline Guest Ranch outside Telluride. Rates include transportation to and from local lodging to the staging area and vary according to the package arranged. Day skiers are provided with lunch.

The guides at Sidewinder Ski Tours have extensive knowledge of the areas they guide and have training in avalanche awareness, first aid and back-country techniques.

Contact Greg Williams, Sidewinder Ski Tours, P.O. Box 1673, Telluride, Co. 81435, (303) 728-4944.

Telluride Helitrax

Telluride Helitrax permit areas are located adjacent to the Wilson and Mt. Sneffels Wilderness, including but not limited to the terrain east of Lizard Head Pass, Waterfall and Swamp canyons near Ophir, and many more areas in the surrounding San Juan and Uncompahgre National Forests. Guides are all certified EMTs and are active avalanche forecasters with strong backgrounds in mountaineering and skiing. These guides act as an avalanche control team for U.S. 550 over Red Mountain Pass.

Several different heliskiing packages are offered. A single lift, giving 1,550 to 3,200 vertical feet of skiing, is available to groups of seven or more skiers for an introduction to heliskiing. Averaging $60 per person, the cost includes a guide and the helicopter lift and safety orientation. This is for intermediate to expert skiers.

Day skiing, for advanced-intermediate through expert skiers, offers 7,500 to 10,000 vertical feet of skiing, and includes four runs, a guide, ground transportation to and from the staging area, a gourmet lunch, and safety orientation for $210. Additional ski runs are available for $25 per run.

Multi-day packages include three days of heliskiing and four nights' lodging at nearby Telluride resorts. Prices start at $800 per person.

High alpine tours are designed for lower intermediate skiers and families ready for a first trip to the high country. In otherwise inaccessible areas, Helitrax offers the confident cross-country skier views of Colorado's most spectacular scenery. Areas commonly visited include Upper South Mineral Creek and Ice Lakes Basin. The high alpine tours provide a guide, a gourmet lunch, transportation to and from the staging area, and safety orientation, and cost $160 per person for a minimum of three skiers.

Helitrax guides are also available for day tours into the wilderness areas surrounding Telluride, where helicopters are not permitted. Rescue beacons, shovels and probe poles are provided. Skiers can find superb ski descents for intermediate-through-expert abilities, ranging from 800 ft. on Back Face to 2,000 ft. at Eldorado. Prices vary according to destination.

Heli-Access Ski Mountaineering to remote mountain sites is available for nordic skiers for $160 per person.

Spring corn-snow excursions for intermediate skiers, offering at least 10,000 vertical feet per day, take place from mid-May to mid-June. During that period, the daily ski, the high alpine tours and ski mountaineering are all offered at reduced spring rates ($195, $140, and $140, respectively).

Rescue beacons are given to each skier at the daily safety orientation, where guides share their safety concerns with skiers. For details on local ski tours or up-to-date avalanche conditions, visit the Helitrax reservation desk (open 4 to 7 p.m. daily) in the lobby of the New Sheridan Hotel in Telluride.

Contact Mike Friedman, Telluride Helitrax, P.O. Box 1560, Telluride, Co. 81435, (303) 728-4904 or 1-(800) 233-9292.

Backcountry Trails

The San Juans are notorious for avalanches, and backcountry skiing without caution and a competent guide is strongly discouraged.

Ridgeway area: East Dallas Road; Big Blue area.

The Ouray Ranger District—Uncompahgre NF, 101 N. Uncompahgre Ave., Montrose, 81401, 249-3711—administers the above.

Telluride area: Lizard Head pass area (EMD); Alta Lakes Trail (M).

The Norwood Ranger District—Uncompahgre NF, E. Grand Ave., Norwood, 81423, 327-4261—administers the above.

Lake City area: Danny Carl Memorial (E); Penniston Park (E); Deer Lakes (MD).

The Cebolla Ranger District—Gunnison NF, 216 N. Colorado, Gunnison, 81230, 641-0471—administers the above.

Silverton area: Molas Lakes area (EMD).

Durango area: Cascade Creek (EM); Chris Park from Bear Ranch (M); Junction Creek (MD); Coalbank Hill (MD); La Plata Canyon (MD); Hermosa Park (D).

The Animas Ranger District—San Juan NF, 701 Camino Del Rio, Rm. 100, Durango, 81301, 259-0195—administers the above. The city of Durango maintains a trail on the Hillcrest Golf Course.

Dolores area: Lizard Head Pass area; Dunton Road; Turkey Flats.

The Dolores Ranger District—San Juan NF, 401 Railroad Ave., Dolores, 81323, 882-7296—administers the above.

Bayfield area: Vallecito Reservoir area; Lemon Reservoir area; Beaver Meadows area; First Fork area.

Pine Ranger District—San Juan NF, 367 S. Pearl St., Bayfield, 81122, 884-2512—administers the above.

Pagosa Springs area: Piedra area.

The Pagosa Ranger District—San Juan NF, Bldg. 180, 2nd and Pagosa, Pagosa Springs, 81147, 264-2268—administers the above.

Wolf Creek Pass area: Big Meadows (M); Tewksberry Creek (M); Largest Tree (M); Cascade Falls (M); Burro Creek (MD); Tucker Ponds (MD); Munger Canyon (D).

The Del Norte Ranger District—Rio Grande National Forest, 810 Grand Ave., Del Norte, 81132, 657-3321—administers the above.

Cumbres Pass—La Manga area: Conejos Plateau, Conejos Canyon, Osier Mountain, and Chama Basin areas. Also the Cat Creek, Jacobs Hill and Rock Creek Archery Range areas.

The Conejos and Alamosa Ranger Districts—Rio Grande National Forest, Highway 285, La Jara, 81140, 274-5193—administer the above.

Creede area: Spring Creek Pass (E); Santa Maria (EM); Weminuche Creek (M); Upper Rio Grande (D). Also the Continental Reservoir, Goose Creek, and Wheeler-Wasson areas.

The Creede Ranger District—Rio Grande National Forest, Creede Ave., Creede, 81130, 658-2556—administers the above.

(E) Easier, (M) Moderate, (D) Difficult.

Appendix

Winter Safety

This appendix contains general guidelines for winter safety. It is recommended that you gain a more thorough understanding of outdoor survival skills by studying books and taking courses on winter safety.

Before you embark on your backcountry trip, know the area you plan to tour, the length of the trail and its degree of difficulty, and your own capabilities. Check weather and avalanche conditions beforehand with a Forest Service ranger. Notify a responsible person of your planned departure and return times and your route of travel. Don't forget to call that person upon your return! Please leave dogs at home when using the trails. Any public-use tents and cabins are on a first-come, first-served basis. Please replace the firewood you use.

Maps

Maps are important tools for backcountry travel, but only if you study them and learn to recognize landmarks. The most detailed topographic maps available are the U.S. Geological Survey 1:24,000 quadrangles, usually sold at local sporting goods stores. If you do not know how to read a "topo" map, ask the salesperson to show you the basics.

A compass with an adjustable base is essential for route finding in poor lighting conditions or a blizzard. The compass needle always points to magnetic north, not true north. The difference between magnetic and true north varies with your geographic location—this is magnetic declination. Adjust the compass for declination according to the compass instructions using the declination given on the map. During travel, when you align the magnetic needle and the orienting arrow in the housing, the direction-of-travel arrow points the way. Be sure to check landmarks on the map as you go.

Eagle Eye Maps publishes a series of Cross-Country Skier's Maps for trails on public lands at a scale of 1:50,000. These maps include information of special interest to the skier. The areas and trails in each backcountry trails section in this book that are covered by an Eagle Eye map are marked with an asterisk. Maps are available in many ski shops or may be ordered by using the form at the back of this book.

A warning: maps should always be used with other sources of information, whether it be a guide or a guidebook. Snowcover and weather can make map reading difficult or impossible at times. **Always** be on the lookout for landmarks.

Clothing and Equipment

Layered clothing, adjustable to varying conditions, is best. Avoid tight-fitting clothing that may cut off circulation. Carry extra clothing, waterproof matches, knife, space blanket, first-aid kit, signal mirror, sunglasses, spare ski tip, metal container (for melting snow), nylon cord, map, compass, high-energy food, and water on each tour.

Food, Water and Sanitation

Food taken on the trip should be high-calorie, but lightweight. Pack enough for meals and emergency rations.

The body loses from two to four quarts of water per day under exertion, so be sure to carry enough water to replace lost fluids. Eating snow drains energy, cools body temperature and provides only limited fluid. If you are short on water, melt snow only if equipped to do so. To avoid contracting giardiasis, an intestinal disorder caused by a micro-organism present in rivers and streams, do not drink untreated natural water. If it is necessary to drink the water, boil it for five minutes at high altitude, or use a special filtration device. Pack out your litter and bury human waste beyond 100 feet of flowing water.

First Aid

Know the causes, symptoms, treatment and prevention of frequent problems encountered during high-altitude and winter activities. Here are some basic guidelines; consult a mountaineering first-aid guide before your trip for more complete information.

Hypothermia is the subnormal temperature of the body leading to mental and physical collapse. It is caused by exposure to cold and is aggravated by wet clothing, wind, and exhaustion.

Uncontrollable fits of shivering, slurred speech, memory lapses, fumbling hands, stumbling, and drowsiness are the symptoms. Most hypothermia cases develop in air temperatures between 30 and 50 degrees. Put on your raingear before you get wet, your warm clothes before you get cold. Stay dry. Forestall exhaustion—carry and nibble on food, or start your return before you tire.

Although the victim may deny he is in trouble, believe the symptoms. Even mild symptoms demand immediate attention, as the victim can slip into a state of hypothermia in minutes. Get the victim out of the rain and wind and strip off all wet clothing. If only mildly impaired, the victim should be given warm drinks. Get him into warm clothes and warm a sleeping bag. If the victim is semi-concious, try to keep him awake. Put the stripped victim in a sleeping bag with another stripped person, as skin-to-skin contact is the most effective treatment. Build a fire if possible.

Altitude sickness can result from travel at high elevations. Lower air pressure and a lower concentration of oxygen can cause listlessness, loss of appetite, weakness, nausea, apathy, dizziness, and drowsiness. Stop, rest, and breathe deeply. Eat simple sugars such as fruit juice, and descend to a lower elevation as soon as possible. To avoid altitude sickness, keep in good physical condition and eat a well-balanced diet. Take a day or two to acclimate to the local elevation before exercise.

Anxiety and high altitude can cause the symptoms of **hyperventilation**: rapid breathing, lightheadedness, and feelings of cold, apprehension and excitability. Calm the victim, and have him breathe into a glove or hat until normal breathing is restored. Avoiding hyperventilation is the same as for altitude sickness.

Exposure of flesh to sub-freezing temperatures can result in a low blood flow to the extremities which causes tissue damage or **frostbite**. The symptoms are a loss of feeling and a dead white appearance to the extremities— nose, ears, fingers and toes especially. Restore the body temperature as rapidly as possible by immersion in a warm-water bath. Keep the affected part covered if it is neccessary to move.

Lost or injured

Avoid becoming lost by using a map and compass and noting landmarks. If you become lost or injured, stay calm. Decide on a plan; backtrack if possible. If this is impractical, stay in place. Build a fire and shelter to keep warm. Stay with your group; if it becomes necessary to send for help, send at least two people. Use distress signals in threes—three shouts, three whistles. Ground-to-air signals can be stamped out in the snow to aid air searches: I (need doctor), II (need medical supplies), F (need food and water),

→ (proceeding in this direction), **N** (negative), **Y** (affirmative), **LL** (all well), **X** (unable to proceed).

Avalanche chute on Red
Mountain Pass.

Avalanches

Avalanches are sudden releases of snow which can occur any time, just about anywhere. Even small avalanches claim lives. It is up to you to be prepared for this situation when you enter the backcountry. The following are basic guidelines; however, a winter mountaineering book or course will give more complete information. (See the *Avalanche Handbook*, Perla and Martinelli, U.S. Dept. of Agriculture Handbook 489.)

There are two types of avalanches: loose snow and slab. Loose snow avalanches start at a point and grow in size—the amount of snow increases as they descend. Slab avalanches start when a large area of snow begins to slide at once—there is a well-defined fracture line where the slab of snow breaks away from the stable snow. Almost all accidents in avalanches are caused by slab avalanches. Many times they are triggered by the victims themselves; the skiers' weight on the snow is enough to break the fragile bonds that hold it to the slope.

Avalanches usually occur where there has been one before. Be on the lookout for avalanche paths. Avoid steep, open, treeless gullies and slopes. If you see new avalanches, suspect dangerous conditions. Clues to danger are snowballs or cartwheels rolling down a slope. If snow on which you are skiing sounds hollow, conditions are probably dangerous. If the snow cracks and the crack continues, slab avalanche danger is high.

Avalanches are most common on slopes of 30- to 45-degree angles, although they can occur on 25- to 60-degree slopes. Slab avalanches are more likely to occur on convex slopes but may also occur on concave slopes. Snow on north-facing slopes is more likely to slide in midwinter, while south-facing slopes are more dangerous in the spring and on sunny days. Leeward slopes are dangerous because of the depth added by wind-deposited snow; windward slopes generally have less snow, which is compacted and can be strong enough to resist movement. Large rocks, trees and brush help to anchor snow, yet avalanches can still start among trees.

A high percentage of all avalanches occur during and shortly after storms. A foot or more of new snow constitutes dangerous conditions. When the old snow depth is sufficient to cover natural anchors such as rocks and brush, additional snow layers will slide more readily.

Sustained winds of 15 miles per hour and over cause avalanche danger to increase rapidly. Snow plumes from ridges and peaks indicate that snow is being moved onto leeward slopes. Snow is unstable under cold temperatures; it settles and stablizes when temperatures are near or above freezing. Rainstorms or spring weather can cause wet snow avalanches; these occur more frequently on south slopes and slopes under exposed rock. Be alert to changes in weather conditions which can cause snowpack adjustments, affect the stability of snow, and trigger avalanches.

Never travel alone. Always check local weather reports and contact the Forest Service ranger for avalanche dangers. If on a valley trail, detour away from snow chutes. When out of the valleys, the safest routes are on ridgetops and slightly on the windward side, away from cornices. If you must cross dangerous slopes, stay high and near the top. Avoid avalanche fracture lines in the snow. Gain ridgetops by detouring around cornice areas. Use areas of dense timber, ridges or rocky outcrops as safety areas. Spend as little time as possible on open slopes.

Only one person at a time should cross a dangerous slope. Remove ski pole straps and ski safety straps, loosen all equipment, put on mittens and hats and fasten all clothing before traveling in avalanche-danger areas. Carry and use an avalanche cord or rescue transceiver.

If you are caught in an avalanche: Discard all equipment. Make swimming (backstroke with legs downslope) motions. Try to stay on top of the snow. Work your way to the side of the avalanche. Get your hands in front of your face and try to make an air space in the snow as you are coming to a stop. Try to remain calm.

If you are the survivor: Mark the place where you last saw the victim. Search for her directly downslope below the last seen point. If she is not on the surface, scuff or probe the snow with a ski pole or stick. Many victims are buried no deeper than two feet. You are the victim's best hope for survival; do not desert her and go for help, unless help is only a few minutes away. After 30 minutes, the buried victim has only a 50-percent chance of surviving. Aid for the victim is the same as for suffocation, shock and hypothermia.

If there is more than one survivor: Send one for help (mark the route) while the others search for the victim. Contact the ski patrol, local sheriff or Forest Service.

The **Avalanche Hotline** in Denver/Boulder is 236-9435, Fort Collins 482-0457, Frisco 668-5485, Vail 827-5687, and Aspen 920-1664. Call before each trip for current information on mountain weather, snow and avalanche conditions, 24 hours/day, November 15 to May 1.

Avalanche danger signs:
• 30- to 45-degree slopes
• No ground cover, bushes or trees
• Cold temperatures (below 32 degrees)
• Convex-shaped slopes
• Needle- or pellet-shaped snow crystals

High avalanche danger signs:
• Sustained winds of 15 mph or greater
• Recent storm (most avalanches occur during or shortly after storms)
• Snowfall at one inch or more per hour

Look out for:
• Recent avalanche activity or snowballs rolling down slopes
• Old slide paths—bent trees, no trees
• Hollow-sounding snow when skied over
• Cracks in snow, cracks continuing to grow
• Smooth surface of old snow under new snow, sun crusts
• Wet snow, free water flowing through snow, on south-facing slopes
• Elevations above timberline (11,500 ft.)

Colorado has established phone numbers that skiers can call for the latest reports on road and skiing conditions. For road conditions, call (303) 639-1111. For skiing conditions at downhill ski areas, which may or may not pertain to skiing conditions at their cross-country ski centers, call (303) 837-9907.

Lisa Stanton lives in Glenwood Springs, Colorado.

Francis Stanton is a freelance cartographer specializing in tourist, illustrative and book maps. He can be reached through Eagle Eye Maps, P.O. Box 1457, Glenwood Springs, Co. 81602.

Caron Elizabeth Dunn is an illustrator and artist, and can be contacted at Illustration and Design, 1942 Broadway, Suite 307, Boulder, Co. 80302.

Louise P. Stanton is an artist living in Illinois.

Order Form

West Side Press
PO Box 1457
Glenwood Springs, CO 81602
(303) 945-8857

Please send me the following publications:

Quan	Name	Amount

_____ COLORADO CROSS-COUNTRY SKIING @$8.95   _____

Cross-Country Skier's Maps of Colorado @$3.95 each:

_____ Frisco-Breckenridge map   _____

_____ Vail-Leadville map   _____

_____ Nederland-Georgetown map   _____

_____ Aspen-Carbondale map   _____

_____ ITEM TOTAL   SUBTOTAL _____

                    Colorado residents please add 6% sales tax _____

                                              Shipping _____

                                              TOTAL _____

Please make check or money order payable to WEST SIDE PRESS.
Shipping: $1.00 for the first item and 25¢ for each additional item.
Satisfaction guaranteed or your money will be refunded in full.

Name _____

Address _____

City _____

State _____ Zip _____ Phone (_____) _____